MANHATTAN PREP

Geometry

GMAT Strategy Guide

This comprehensive guide illustrates every geometric principle, formula, and problem type tested on the GMAT. Understand and master the intricacies of shapes, planes, lines, angles, and objects.

guide **4**

Geometry GMAT Strategy Guide, Sixth Edition

10-digit International Standard Book Number: 1-941234-03-8
13-digit International Standard Book Number: 978-1-941234-03-7
eISBN: 978-1-941234-24-2

Note: *GMAT, Graduate Management Admission Test, Graduate Management Admission
Council,* and *GMAC* are all registered trademarks of the Graduate Management
Admission Council, which neither sponsors nor is affiliated in any way with this product.

Layout Design: Dan McNaney and Cathy Huang
Cover Design: Dan McNaney and Frank Callaghan
Cover Photography: Alli Ugosoli

INSTRUCTIONAL GUIDE SERIES

0 GMAT Roadmap
(ISBN: 978-1-941234-09-9)

1 Fractions, Decimals, & Percents
(ISBN: 978-1-941234-02-0)

2 Algebra
(ISBN: 978-1-941234-00-6)

3 Word Problems
(ISBN: 978-1-941234-08-2)

4 Geometry
(ISBN: 978-1-941234-03-7)

5 Number Properties
(ISBN: 978-1-941234-05-1)

6 Critical Reasoning
(ISBN: 978-1-941234-01-3)

7 Reading Comprehension
(ISBN: 978-1-941234-06-8)

8 Sentence Correction
(ISBN: 978-1-941234-07-5)

9 Integrated Reasoning & Essay
(ISBN: 978-1-941234-04-4)

SUPPLEMENTAL GUIDE SERIES

Math GMAT Supplement Guides

Foundations of GMAT Math
(ISBN: 978-1-935707-59-2)

Advanced GMAT Quant
(ISBN: 978-1-935707-15-8)

Official Guide Companion
(ISBN: 978-0-984178-01-8)

Verbal GMAT Supplement Guides

Foundations of GMAT Verbal
(ISBN: 978-1-935707-01-9)

Official Guide Companion for Sentence Correction
(ISBN: 978-1-937707-41-5)

MANHATTAN
PREP

December 2nd, 2014

Dear Student,

Thank you for picking up a copy of *Geometry*. I hope this book gives you just the guidance you need to get the most out of your GMAT studies.

A great number of people were involved in the creation of the book you are holding. First and foremost is Zeke Vanderhoek, the founder of Manhattan Prep. Zeke was a lone tutor in New York City when he started the company in 2000. Now, well over a decade later, the company contributes to the successes of thousands of students around the globe every year.

Our Manhattan Prep Strategy Guides are based on the continuing experiences of our instructors and students. The overall vision of the 6th Edition GMAT guides was developed by Stacey Koprince, Whitney Garner, and Dave Mahler over the course of many months; Stacey and Dave then led the execution of that vision as the primary author and editor, respectively, of this book. Numerous other instructors made contributions large and small, but I'd like to send particular thanks to Josh Braslow, Kim Cabot, Dmitry Farber, Ron Purewal, Emily Meredith Sledge, and Ryan Starr. Dan McNaney and Cathy Huang provided design and layout expertise as Dan managed book production, while Liz Krisher made sure that all the moving pieces, both inside and outside of our company, came together at just the right time. Finally, we are indebted to all of the Manhattan Prep students who have given us feedback over the years. This book wouldn't be half of what it is without your voice.

At Manhattan Prep, we aspire to provide the best instructors and resources possible, and we hope that you will find our commitment manifest in this book. We strive to keep our books free of errors, but if you think we've goofed, please post to manhattanprep.com/GMAT/errata. If you have any questions or comments in general, please email our Student Services team at gmat@manhattanprep.com. Or give us a shout at 212-721-7400 (or 800-576-4628 in the U.S. or Canada). I look forward to hearing from you.

Thanks again, and best of luck preparing for the GMAT!

Sincerely,

Chris Ryan
Vice President of Academics
Manhattan Prep

HOW TO ACCESS YOUR ONLINE RESOURCES

IF YOU ARE A REGISTERED MANHATTAN PREP STUDENT

and have received this book as part of your course materials, you have AUTOMATIC access to ALL of our online resources. This includes all practice exams, question banks, and online updates to this book. To access these resources, follow the instructions in the Welcome Guide provided to you at the start of your program. Do NOT follow the instructions below.

IF YOU PURCHASED THIS BOOK FROM MANHATTANPREP.COM OR AT ONE OF OUR CENTERS

1. Go to: **www.manhattanprep.com/gmat/studentcenter**
2. Log in with the username and password you chose when setting up your account.

IF YOU PURCHASED THIS BOOK AT A RETAIL LOCATION

1. Go to: **www.manhattanprep.com/gmat/access**
2. Create an account or, if you already have one, log in on this page with your username and password.
3. Follow the instructions on the screen.

Your one year of online access begins on the day that you register your book at the above URL.

You only need to register your product ONCE at the above URL. To use your online resources any time AFTER you have completed the registration process, log in to the following URL:

www.manhattanprep.com/gmat/studentcenter

Please note that online access is nontransferable. This means that only NEW and UNREGISTERED copies of the book will grant you online access. Previously used books will NOT provide any online resources.

IF YOU PURCHASED AN EBOOK VERSION OF THIS BOOK

1. Create an account with Manhattan Prep at this website:

www.manhattanprep.com/gmat/register

2. Email a copy of your purchase receipt to **gmat@manhattanprep.com** to activate your resources. Please be sure to use the same email address to create an account that you used to purchase the eBook.

For any questions, email **gmat@manhattanprep.com** or call **800-576-4628**.

Please refer to the following page for a description of the online resources that come with this book.

YOUR ONLINE RESOURCES
YOUR PURCHASE INCLUDES ONLINE ACCESS TO THE FOLLOWING:

6 FULL-LENGTH GMAT PRACTICE EXAMS

The 6 full-length GMAT practice exams included with the purchase of this book are delivered online using Manhattan Prep's proprietary computer-adaptive test engine. The exams adapt to your ability level by drawing from a bank of more than 1,200 unique questions of varying difficulty levels written by Manhattan Prep's expert instructors, all of whom have scored in the 99th percentile on the Official GMAT. At the end of each exam you will receive a score, an analysis of your results, and the opportunity to review detailed explanations for each question. You may choose to take the exams timed or untimed.

Important Note: The 6 GMAT exams included with the purchase of this book are the SAME exams that you receive upon purchasing ANY book in the Manhattan Prep GMAT Complete Strategy Guide Set.

5 FREE INTERACT™ LESSONS

Interact™ is a comprehensive self-study program that is fun, intuitive, and directed by you. Each interactive video lesson is taught by an expert Manhattan Prep instructor and includes dozens of individual branching points. The choices you make define the content you see. This book comes with access to the first five lessons of GMAT Interact. Lessons are available on your computer or iPad so you can prep where you are, when you want. For more information on the full version of this program, visit **manhattanprep.com/gmat/interact**

GEOMETRY ONLINE QUESTION BANK

The Online Question Bank for Geometry consists of 25 extra practice questions (with detailed explanations) that test the variety of concepts and skills covered in this book. These questions provide you with extra practice beyond the problem sets contained in this book. You may use our online timer to practice your pacing by setting time limits for each question in the bank.

ONLINE UPDATES TO THE CONTENT IN THIS BOOK

The content presented in this book is updated periodically to ensure that it reflects the GMAT's most current trends. You may view all updates, including any known errors or changes, upon registering for online access.

The above resources can be found in your Student Center at manhattanprep.com/gmat/studentcenter

TABLE *of* CONTENTS

guide **4**

Official Guide Problem Sets

As you work through this strategy guide, it is a very good idea to test your skills using official problems that appeared on the real GMAT in the past. To help you with this step of your studies, we have classified all of the problems from the three main *Official Guide* books and devised some problem sets to accompany this book.

These problem sets live in your Manhattan Prep Student Center so that they can be updated whenever the test makers update their books. When you log into your Student Center, click on the link for the *Official Guide Problem Sets*, found on your home page. Download them today!

The problem sets consist of four broad groups of questions:

1. A mid-term quiz: Take this quiz after completing **Chapter 4** of this guide.

2. A final quiz: Take this quiz after completing this entire guide.

3. A full practice set of questions: If you are taking one of our classes, this is the home-work given on your syllabus, so just follow the syllabus assignments. If you are not taking one of our classes, you can do this practice set whenever you feel that you have a very solid understanding of the material taught in this guide.

4. A full reference list of all *Official Guide* problems that test the topics covered in this strategy guide: Use these problems to test yourself on specific topics or to create larger sets of mixed questions.

As you begin studying, try one problem at a time and review it thoroughly before moving on. In the middle of your studies, attempt some mixed sets of problems from a small pool of topics (the two quizzes we've devised for you are good examples of how to do this). Later in your studies, mix topics from multiple guides and include some questions that you've chosen randomly out of the *Official Guide*. This way, you'll learn to be prepared for anything!

Study Tips:

1. DO time yourself when answering questions.

2. DO cut yourself off and make a guess if a question is taking too long. You can try it again later without a time limit, but first practice the behavior you want to exhibit on the real test: let go and move on.

3. DON'T answer all of the *Official Guide* questions by topic or chapter at once. The real test will toss topics at you in random order, and half of the battle is figuring out what each new question is testing. Set yourself up to learn this when doing practice sets.

Chapter 1 *of* Geometry

Geometry Strategy

In This Chapter...

Chapter 1
Geometry Strategy

Welcome to your *Geometry Strategy Guide*—and everything you ever wanted to know about geometry (as it's tested on the GMAT, anyway). Before diving into the rules and formulas, take a few minutes to learn some important strategies that will help you on every Geometry problem you will do on the real test.

The Three Principles

Use three general principles to succeed on Geometry problems:

1. If they don't tell you, don't assume.

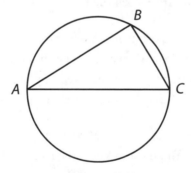

> Points *A*, *B*, and *C* lie on the circle and form a triangle. Is line segment *AC* a
> diameter of the circle?

Line segment *AC* does look like a diameter of the circle, but it could be just slightly off and not a diameter at all. Don't make any assumptions; just *looking* like a diameter doesn't make *AC* a diameter on the GMAT.

Vocab Lesson: when a triangle lies inside a circle and the "points" (or *vertices*) of a triangle touch the circle, then the triangle is said to be *inscribed* in the circle.

1

2. If they give you a piece of information, use it.

Given: line segment *AC* passes through the center of the circle.

What can you infer from that piece of information?

If a line segment passes from one side to the other of a circle through the center, then that line segment must be a diameter of the circle. Now, you've got a connection between the triangle and the circle: the longest side of the triangle is also a diameter of the circle.

How does that help? Read on—but note that, any time you're given multiple shapes, the trick to solving the problem usually revolves around finding connections between those shapes.

3. Know your rules and formulas.

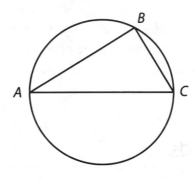

Rule:

If one of the sides of a triangle inscribed in a circle
is a diameter of the circle, then the triangle must be a right triangle.

Translation necessary! If you inscribe a triangle in a circle (as in the figure shown above), and one side of that triangle is also a diameter of the circle, then angle *B* has to be a right angle. It doesn't matter where you place *B* on the circle; it will still be a right angle. (Well, if you place *B* right on *A* or *C*, then *B* won't be a right angle. In that case, though, *ABC* also won't be a triangle!)

In short, it is not enough just to memorize a bunch of rules. The test writers are going to "cut up" the rules and give them to you in pieces. You need to know the rules well enough that you can put those pieces back together.

To recap:

1. If they don't tell you, don't assume.

2. If they give you a piece of information, use it.

3. Know your rules and formulas.

MANHATTAN
PREP

One last thing: it turns out, thankfully, that there are a few small things you *can* take for granted on GMAT Geometry.

If the problem describes a shape as a triangle, then it really is a triangle. If the problem discusses a line, then you really do have a 180° straight line. In other words, you can take the test at its word—it will use the word *line* in the official geometry sense—but you can't add in any extra assumptions.

Figures on Problem-Solving questions will be drawn to scale unless noted. Any points shown on a figure or number line do appear in the order shown. For instance, consider the figure below:

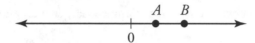

You can trust that both *A* and *B* are positive (because both are shown to the right of 0) and that *B* is greater than *A* (because *B* is to the right of *A*).

Figures on Data-Sufficiency questions, however, are *not* necessarily drawn to scale (and they will *not* be noted accordingly). You can trust that lines are lines, and that intersecting lines or shapes do intersect, including the relative positions of points, angles, and regions. Other than that, anything goes.

The Three-Step Approach

On all Quant problems, you're going to use a three-step approach to solving, as depicted in the figure below:

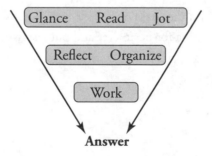

Your first task is to figure out what you've got. This will include a couple of special steps for Geometry problems.

1. Glance, read, jot: draw everything on your scrap paper.

Glance at the problem: is it problem solving or data sufficiency? Are there any figures or obvious formulas?

As you read, jot down any obvious information. If the problem gives you a formula, write it down. If it gives you a figure, redraw it on your scrap paper. If it doesn't, but it's a geometry problem, draw one anyway.

You have graph paper, so make the figure decently precise. Don't waste time or space, of course, but make the figure big enough that you can see what you're doing and accurate enough to prevent careless mistakes. For instance, if you know one side of a triangle is larger than another, draw the figure so that the longer side *looks* longer.

Add to the figure as you work. Every time you infer something new, write or draw it in. (Make sure, when you first draw the figure, that you give yourself enough space to draw and write additional information on it!)

Also, off to the side, write down any formulas that are mentioned in the problem. For example, if the problem mentions the area of a circle, immediately write $A = \pi r^2$ next to the figure.

2. Reflect, organize: identify the "wanted" element.

Don't dive into the calculations quite yet. Figure out what you need, first. Perhaps the question asks you to find the measure of angle x, which has already been labeled on the figure. Put a symbol, such as a star, next to the x to remind yourself that this is your goal. (You can use any symbol you want, as long as you use the same symbol consistently and as long as you use a symbol that will never be used by the test writers themselves.)

Perhaps the question asks you to find the perimeter of a rectangle. It would be tough to show that on the figure, so instead, write the formula for perimeter and put a star next to the P:

$$\star P = 2l + 2w$$

Alternatively, write something like:

$$P = \underline{\hspace{2cm}}\,?$$

You have flexibility in terms of how you decide to show this information, however, you should develop a consistent method for noting what the question wants.

Finally, take a look at what you've been given. What possible solution paths come to mind? Choose one and…

1

3. Work: infer from the given information.

The "givens," or starting information, will allow you to deduce certain other things that must be true. Your task is to figure out the path from those givens to the answer.

Do you remember doing geometry proofs in school? You were given two or three starting points and had to prove, in a certain number of steps, that some other piece of information was true. People generally don't like proofs because it feels as though there are a million different ways that you could try to complete the proof.

GMAT questions can feel that way, too, but don't let that feeling demoralize you. On the vast majority of Geometry questions, you won't have to take more than three or four steps to find your way to the answer.

Try out the three-step process on this problem:

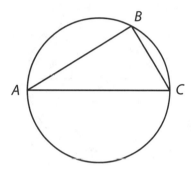

Triangle *ABC* is inscribed in the circle and line *AC* passes through the center of the circle. If the length of line segment *AB* is 3 and the length of line segment *AC* is 5, then what is the length of line segment *BC*?

(A) 2
(B) 3
(C) 4
(D) 6
(E) 8

1

1. Glance, read, jot

Draw the figure on your scrap paper and add the given lengths:

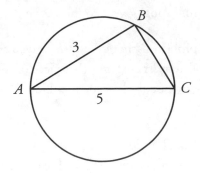

2. Reflect, organize

Time to start thinking! What do they want? The length of line *BC*—add that to your figure:

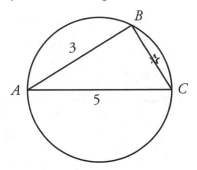

What else should you think about? Usually, when the figure has multiple shapes, the solution will hinge upon some connection between those shapes.

3. Work

Bingo! Since line segment *AC* passes through the center of the circle, line segment *AC* must be a diameter of the circle. The two shapes are connected. What else can you infer?

Given that *AC* is a diameter, *ABC* must be a right triangle and angle *B* must be the right angle. Great! You can use the Pythagorean theorem to solve!

$$a^2 + b^2 = c^2$$
$$3^2 + b^2 = 5^2$$
$$9 + b^2 = 25$$
$$b^2 = 16$$
$$b = 4$$

The correct answer is 4.

Now, don't worry if you've completely forgotten about the Pythagorean theorem or any of the other math needed to answer this question. You'll re-learn how to do it all while working through this book.

Estimation

You can estimate your way to an answer on problems with certain characteristics; this technique is often helpful on Geometry problems in particular.

First, it's important that the problem gives you either a figure drawn to scale or enough information to draw a figure reasonably to scale yourself. Remember that your scrap paper will be graph paper, so you can draw right angles, squares, and other dimensions reasonably accurately.

Second, the answers need to be spread far enough apart that estimating an answer will still keep you in the range of the one correct answer.

For instance, say you are given these answer choices:

(A) 25°

(B) 45°

(C) 60°

(D) 90°

(E) 110°

You might not know how to calculate the correct answer, but you might be able to tell, for example, that the desired angle is less than 90°, which will eliminate (D) and (E). Alternatively, you might be able to tell that the answer is close to 90°, allowing you to chop out (A) and (B), and possibly (C).

This technique can be used on any Problem Solving problem (not just Geometry!) in which the answers are spread far apart, though on Geometry, you also benefit from a figure that's reasonably to scale.

Try this problem, inspired by one from *The Official Guide for GMAT Review 2015*:

A square has a 10-centimeter diagonal. What is the area of the square, in centimeters?

(A)   50
(B)   64
(C)   100
(D)   144
(E)   200

First, draw a square on your scrap paper. Remember, you'll have graph paper, so you can make a true square. Draw a diagonal and label it 10:

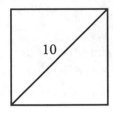

The area of a square is s^2, where s is the length of one side. Because the diagonal is 10, the length of one side must be less than 10. If the length of a side were 10, then the area would be 10^2, which equals 100, so if the length is less than 10, then the area must also be less than 100. Eliminate answers (C), (D), and (E). There are only two answers left!

You might be thinking, "that's too good to be true… the real test won't do that." It does; in fact, this problem is based on a real question from a past official exam. If you have a copy of the *Official Guide 2015*, feel free to try Problem Solving question #104 right now.

You may also be thinking: I can already answer this problem; why would I estimate to make a guess?

First, you learn how to estimate on harder problems by practicing the skill on easier ones, so if you find this problem easy, don't dismiss the idea of estimating.

Second, you can use the rough estimation to check your work. Say that you made a calculation error and called the length of one side $10\sqrt{2}$. (There is a specific reason why someone might be susceptible to that particular mistake! If you're not sure what it is, look at this problem again after you've studied Chapter 4, Triangles & Diagonals.)

If you call one side $10\sqrt{2}$, then you're going to calculate the area as 200, which is answer (E). If you then double-check your work via estimation, you'll realize that 200 is too big.

The online *Official Guide* Problem Sets that come with this guide offer some additional *OG* problems on which you can test your estimation skills.

Get Started!

Start using the following three-step approach on all Quant problems:

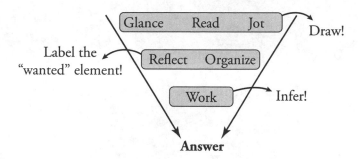

Remember to draw figures, label what you're looking for, and only then think about solving. Infer from the information given.

While you're working, avoid making assumptions. Make sure to use the information they give you. Finally, if you don't know the rules and formulas, it will be very tough to solve; make sure you know your rules!

You're ready to dive into Geometry. Good luck!

Problem Set

If you think you remember some (or many!) geometry rules, use this problem set as a quiz to see where you need to review. If, on the other hand, you've totally forgotten all of your geometry rules, skip this set for now and come back to the problems after working through the relevant chapters in this book.

1. If the length of an edge of cube A is one-third the length of an edge of cube B, what is the ratio of the volume of cube A to the volume of cube B?

2.

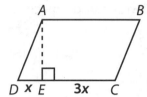

    ABCD is a parallelogram (see figure above). The ratio of DE to EC is 1 : 3. Height AE has a length of 3. If quadrilateral ABCE has an area of 21, what is the area of ABCD?

3.

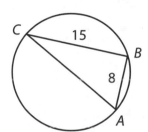

    Triangle ABC is inscribed in a circle, such that AC is a diameter of the circle (see figure above). If AB has a length of 8 and BC has a length of 15, what is the circumference of the circle?

4. Triangle ABC is inscribed in a circle, such that AC is a diameter of the circle and angle BAC is 45°. If the area of triangle ABC is 72 square units, how much larger is the area of the circle than the area of triangle ABC?

5. ![number line with x, y, z]

    On the number line above, is $xy < 0$?

    (1) Zero is to the left of y on the number line above.

    (2) xy and yz have opposite signs.

1

6.

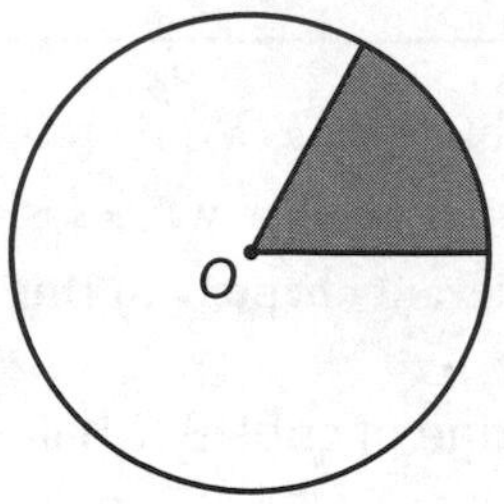

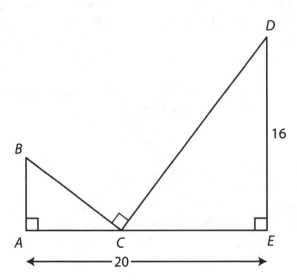

In the figure above, if *O* represents the center of a circular clock and the point of the clock hand is on the circumference of the circle, does the shaded sector of the clock represent more than 10 minutes?

    (1) The clock hand has a length of 10.

    (2) The area of the sector is greater than 16π.

7.

What is the area of triangle *ABC* (see figure above)?

    (1) $DC = 20$

    (2) $AC = 8$

8. The side of an equilateral triangle has the same length as the diagonal of a square. What is the area of the square?

    (1) The height of the equilateral triangle is equal to $6\sqrt{3}$.

    (2) The area of the equilateral triangle is equal to $36\sqrt{3}$.

MANHATTAN
PREP

9.

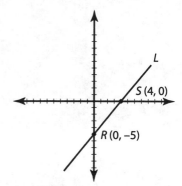

Line L passes through points R (0, −5) and S (4, 0) (see figure above). Point P with coordinates (x, y) is a point on line L. Is $xy > 0$?

(1) $x > 4$

(2) $y > -5$

Solutions

1. **1 to 27:** There are no specified amounts in this question, so pick numbers. You can say that cube A has sides of length 1 and cube B has sides of length 3:

> Volume of cube A = 1 × 1 × 1 = 1
> Volume of cube B = 3 × 3 × 3 = 27

Therefore, the ratio of the volume of cube A to the volume of cube B is $\frac{1}{27}$, or 1 : 27.

2. **24:** First, break quadrilateral *ABCE* into two pieces: a 3 by 3*x* rectangle and a right triangle with a base of *x* and a height of 3. Therefore, the area of quadrilateral *ABCE* is given by the following equation:

$$(3 \times 3x) + \frac{3 \times x}{2} = 9x + 1.5x = 10.5x$$

If *ABCE* has an area of 21, then 21 = 10.5*x*, which reduces to *x* = 2. Quadrilateral *ABCD* is a parallelogram, so you can use the formula for area: *A* = (base) × (height), or 4*x* × 3. Substitute the known value of 2 for *x* and simplify:

$$A = 4(2) \times 3 = 24$$

3. **17π:** If line segment *AC* is a diameter of the circle, then inscribed triangle *ABC* is a right triangle, with *AC* as the hypotenuse. Therefore, you can apply the Pythagorean Theorem to find the length of *AC*:

$$
\begin{aligned}
8^2 + 15^2 &= c^2 \\
64 + 225 &= c^2 \\
289 &= c^2 \\
c &= 17
\end{aligned}
$$

You might also have recognized the common 8–15–17 right triangle.

The circumference of the circle is π*d*, or 17π.

4. **72π − 72:** If *AC* is a diameter of the circle, then angle *ABC* is a right angle. Therefore, triangle *ABC* is a 45–45–90 triangle, and the base and the height are equal. Assign the variable *x* to represent both the base and height:

$$
\begin{aligned}
A &= \frac{bh}{2} \\
72 &= \frac{(x)(x)}{2} \\
144 &= x^2 \\
x &= 12
\end{aligned}
$$

Because this is a 45–45–90 triangle, and the two legs are equal to 12, the common ratio tells you that the hypotenuse, which is also the diameter of the circle, is $12\sqrt{2}$. Therefore, the radius is equal to $6\sqrt{2}$ and the area of the circle, πr^2, equals 72π. The area of the circle is $72\pi - 72$ square units larger than the area of triangle ABC.

5. **(C):** First, note that this is a Yes/No Data Sufficiency question.

For xy to be negative, x and y need to have opposite signs. On the number line shown, this would only happen if 0 falls between x and y. If 0 is to the left of x on the number line shown, both x and y would be positive, so $xy > 0$. If 0 is to the right of y on the number line shown, both x and y would be negative, so $xy > 0$.

(1) INSUFFICIENT: If zero is to the left of y on the number line, zero could be between x and y. Thus, $xy < 0$ and the answer to the question is yes. However, if 0 is to the left of x, both x and y would be positive, so $xy > 0$ and the answer is no.

(2) INSUFFICIENT: xy and yz having opposite signs implies that one of the three variables has a different sign than the other two. If x, y, and z all have the same sign, xy and yz would have the same sign. Thus, this statement implies that 0 does not fall to the left of x (which would make all three variables, as well as xy and yz, positive) nor to the right of z (which would make all three variables negative, and both xy and yz positive). The only two cases this statement allows are:

> Zero is between x and y: yz is positive and xy is negative (the answer is "yes").
> Zero is between y and z: yz is negative and xy is positive (the answer is "no").

(1) AND (2) SUFFICIENT: Statement (1) restricts 0 to left of y on the number line. This rules out one of the two cases allowed by statement (2), leaving only the case in which 0 is between x and y. Thus, xy is negative, and the answer is a definite yes.

The correct answer is **(C)**.

6. **(E):** First, note that this is a Yes/No Data Sufficiency question.

The question "Does the shaded sector of the clock represent more than 10 minutes?" is really asking you about the area of a sector of a circle.

Since 10 minutes is $\frac{1}{6}$ of an hour, you are being asked if the shaded region is equal to more than $\frac{1}{6}$ of the area of the circle.

(1) INSUFFICIENT: The "clock hand" is equal to the radius. Knowing that the radius equals 10 is enough to tell you that the entire area of the circle is equal to 100π. You can rephrase the question as, "Is the area of the shaded region more than one-sixth of 100π?" You can simplify $\frac{1}{6}$ of 100π as such:

$$\frac{100\pi}{6} = \frac{50\pi}{3} = 16.\overline{6}\pi$$

Thus, the question can be rephrased as, "Is the area of the shaded region more than $16.\overline{6}\pi$?" However, you don't know anything about the area of the shaded region from this statement alone.

(2) INSUFFICIENT: The area of the sector is more than 16π. By itself, this does not tell you anything about whether the area of the sector is more than $\frac{1}{6}$ the area of the circle, since you do not know the area of the entire circle.

(1) AND (2) INSUFFICIENT: The area of the entire circle is 100π, and the area of the sector is "more than 16π."

Since $\frac{1}{6}$ of the area of the circle is actually $16.\overline{6}\pi$, knowing that the area of the sector is "more than 16π" is still insufficient—the area of the sector could be 16.1π or something much larger.

The correct answer is **(E)**.

7. **(D):** First, note that this is a Value Data Sufficiency question.

A big mistake in this problem would be to plunge into the statements without fully analyzing and exploiting the figure. You've got two right triangles that share a 90° span on either side of point C. What's going on here?

As it turns out, *these triangles are similar*.

Any time two triangles *each* have a right angle and *also* share an additional right angle (or, in this case, the 90° span at point C), they will be similar. But if you didn't know that, you could easily uncover that fact by labeling any angle as x and labeling the others in terms of x:

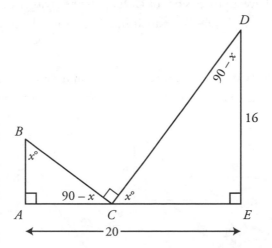

Once you determine that both triangles have the angles 90°, x, and $90 - x$, you may wish to redraw one or both of them in order to get them facing in the same direction.

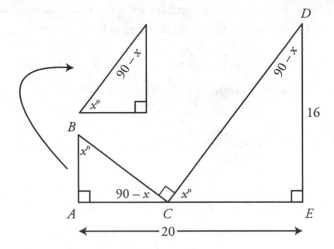

Now, decide exactly what the question is asking. You need the area of triangle *ABC*. In order to get that, you need the base and height of that triangle.

Since the two triangles are right triangles, if you had any two sides of triangle *ABC*, you could get the third. Because the two triangles are similar, you could use any two sides of triangle *CDE* (note that you already have that side *DE* = 16), as well as the ratio of one triangle's size to the other, to get the third side of *CDE* as well as all three sides of *ABC*.

Thus, the rephrased question is, "What are any two sides of *ABC*, or what is any additional side of *CDE* plus the ratio of the size of each triangle to the other?"

(1) SUFFICIENT: Side *DC* equals 20. Use the 20 and the 16 to get, via the Pythagorean theorem, that side *CE* equals 12 (or simply recognize that you have a multiple of a 3–4–5 triangle). If *CE* equals 12 then *AC* equals 8. Thus, you have all three sides of *CDE*, plus the ratio of one triangle to the other (side *AC*, which equals 8, matches up with side *DE*, which equals 16; thus the smaller triangle is one-half the side of the larger).

Note that it is totally unnecessary to calculate further (once you have correctly rephrased the question, don't waste time doing more than is needed to answer the rephrase!), but if you are curious:

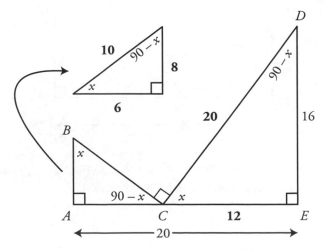

MANHATTAN
PREP

(2) SUFFICIENT: Side *AC* equals 8. Note that this gives you the same information as Statement 1. If *AC* equals 8, then *CE* equals 12 and you can calculate all three sides of *CDE*. Once you know that side *AC* equals 8 and that *AC* matches up with *DE*, which is equal to 16, you can know all three sides of *ABC*, as above.

The correct answer is **(D)**.

8. **(D):** No calculation is needed to solve this problem. Both equilateral triangles and squares are *regular figures*—those that can change size, but never shape.

Regular figures (squares, equilaterals, circles, spheres, cubes, 45–45–90 triangles, 30–60–90 triangles, and others) are those for which you only need one measurement to know *every* measurement. For instance, if you have the radius of a circle, you can get the diameter, circumference, and area. If you have a 45–45–90 or 30–60–90 triangle, you only need *one* side to get all three. In this problem, if you have the side of an equilateral, you could get the height, area, and perimeter. If you have the side of a square, you could get the diagonal, area, and perimeter.

If you have *two* regular figures, as you do in this problem, and you know how they are related numerically ("the side of an equilateral triangle has the same length as the diagonal of a square"), then you can safely conclude that *any* measurement for *either* figure will give you *any* measurement for either figure.

The question can be rephrased as, *"What is the length of any part of either figure?"*

  (1) This gives you the height of the triangle. SUFFICIENT.
  (2) This gives you the area of the triangle. SUFFICIENT.

If you really wanted to "prove" that the answer is (D), you could waste a lot of time:

From statement 1, if the height of the equilateral is $6\sqrt{3}$, then the side equals 12, because heights and sides of equilaterals always exist in that ratio (the height is always one-half the side times $\sqrt{3}$). Then you would know that the diagonal of the square was also equal to 12, and from there you could use the 45–45–90 formula to conclude that the side of the square was $\dfrac{12}{\sqrt{2}}$, and therefore that the area was $\dfrac{144}{2}$, or 72.

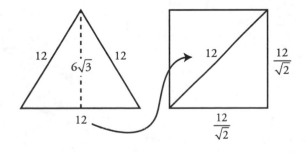

1

Similarly, from statement 2, you could conclude that if the area of the triangle is $36\sqrt{3}$, then the base times the height is $72\sqrt{3}$, and that since the side and height of an equilateral always exist in a fixed ratio (as above, the height is always one-half the side times $\sqrt{3}$), that the side is 12 and the height is $6\sqrt{3}$. Then, as above, you would know that the diagonal of the square was also equal to 12, and from there you could use the 45–45–90 formula to conclude that the side of the square was $\dfrac{12}{\sqrt{2}}$, and therefore that the area was $\dfrac{144}{2}$, or 72.

Who's got the time? This is a logic problem more than it is a math problem. If you understand the logic behind *regular figures*, you can answer this question in under 30 seconds with no math whatsoever.

The correct answer is (D).

9. **(A):** First, note that this is a Yes/No Data Sufficiency question.

Line L passes through three quadrants:

1. Quadrant I, where x and y are both positive, so $xy > 0$ and the answer is yes.
2. Quadrant III, where x and y are both negative, so $xy > 0$ and the answer is yes.
3. Quadrant IV, where x is positive and y is negative, so $xy < 0$ and the answer is no.

If you can determine what quadrant point P is in, you will have sufficient information to answer the question. Also, if you know that point P is in either Quadrant I or Quadrant III, that would also be sufficient.

(1) SUFFICIENT: If $x > 4$, then point P is in Quadrant I, so $xy > 0$ and the answer is "yes."

(2) INSUFFICIENT: If $y > -5$, then point P could be in either Quadrant I ($xy > 0$) or Quadrant IV ($xy < 0$).

The correct answer is (A).

Chapter 2

of Geometry

Lines & Angles

In This Chapter...

Chapter 2

Lines & Angles

A straight line is the shortest distance between two points. As an angle, a line measures 180°.

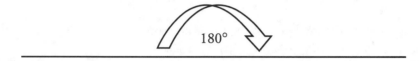

Parallel lines are lines that lie in a plane and that never intersect. No matter how far you extend the lines, they never meet. Two parallel lines are shown below:

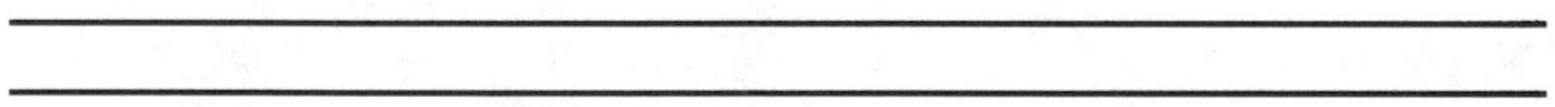

Perpendicular lines are lines that intersect at a 90° angle. Two perpendicular lines are shown below:

There are two major line–angle relationships to know for the GMAT. You'll learn about both in this chapter:

1. The angles formed by any intersecting lines
2. The angles formed by parallel lines cut by a transversal

Intersecting Lines

Intersecting lines have three important properties.

First, the interior angles formed by intersecting lines form a circle, so the sum of these angles is 360°. In the figure to the right: $a + b + c + d = 360$.

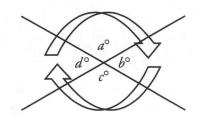

Second, interior angles that combine to form a line sum to 180°. Thus, in the figure shown, $a + b = 180$, because angles a and b form a line together. Other pairs of angles are $b + c = 180$, $c + d = 180$, and $d + a = 180$.

Third, angles found opposite each other where two lines intersect are equal. These are called **vertical angles**. Thus, in the figure above, $a = c$, because these angles are opposite each other and are formed from the same two lines. Additionally, $b = d$ for the same reason.

Note that these rules apply to more than two lines that intersect at a point, as shown to the right. In this figure, $a + b + c + d + e + f = 360$, because these angles combine to form a circle. In addition, $a + b + c = 180$, because these three angles combine to form a line. Finally, $a = d$, $b = e$, and $c = f$, because they are pairs of vertical angles.

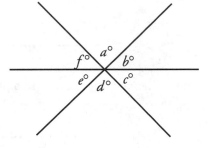

Parallel Lines Cut By a Transversal

The GMAT makes frequent use of figures that include parallel lines cut by a **transversal**.

Notice that there are eight angles formed by this construction, but there are only two *different* angle measures (a and b). All the **acute** angles (less than 90°) in this figure are equal. Likewise, all the **obtuse** angles (greater than 90° but less than 180°) are equal. Any acute angle plus any obtuse angle equals 180°.

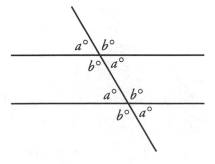

Thus, $a + b = 180$.

MANHATTAN
PREP

When you see a transversal cutting two lines that you know to be parallel, fill in all the *a* (acute) and *b* (obtuse) angles, as in the figure on the previous page.

Sometimes the GMAT disguises the parallel lines and the transversal so that they are not readily apparent, as in the figure to the right. In these disguised cases, extend the lines so that you can more easily see the parallel lines and the transversal, as in the second figure. Label the acute and obtuse angles. You might also mark the parallel lines with arrows, as shown in the figure, in order to indicate that the two lines are parallel.

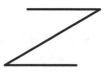

The GMAT uses the symbol ‖ to indicate in text that two lines or line segments are parallel. For instance, if you see *MN* ‖ *OP* in a problem, you know that line segment *MN* is parallel to line segment *OP*.

Problem Set

Problems 1–2 refer to the figure to the right, where line *AB* is parallel to line *CD*.

1. If $x - y = 10$, what is x?

2. If $x + (x + y) = 320$, what is x?

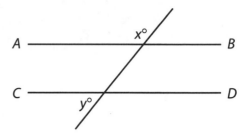

Problems 3–4 refer to the figure to the right.

3. If a is 95, what is $b + d - e$?

4. If $c + f = 70$, and $d = 80$, what is b?

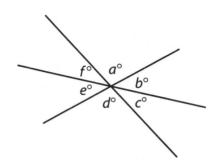

Problems 5–7 refer to the figure to the right.

5. If $c + g = 140$, find k.

6. If $g = 90$, what is $a + k$?

7. If $f + k = 150$, find b.

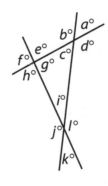

Solutions

1. **95°:** You know that $x + y = 180$, since the figure is a transversal cutting across two parallel lines, in which any acute angle plus any obtuse angle equals 180. Add the two equations together to eliminate the y variable and solve for x:

$$\begin{aligned} x + y &= 180 \\ + \quad x - y &= 10 \\ \hline 2x &= 190 \\ x &= 95 \end{aligned}$$

2. **140°:** Subtract the equation $x + y = 180$ from $2x + y = 320$ to eliminate y and solve for x:

$$\begin{aligned} 2x + y &= 320 \\ - \quad (x + y &= 180) \\ \hline x &= 140 \end{aligned}$$

Don't forget to *subtract* each element in the second line.

Alternatively, because you know that $x + y = 180$, you can substitute this into the given equation of $x + (x + y) = 320$ to solve for x:

$$\begin{aligned} x + 180 &= 320 \\ x &= 140 \end{aligned}$$

3. **95°:** Because a and d are vertical angles, they have the same measure: $a = d = 95$. Likewise, since b and e are vertical angles, they have the same measure: $b = e$. Therefore, $b + d - e = b + d - b = d = 95$.

4. **65°:** Because c and f are vertical angles, they have the same measure: $c + f = 70$, so $c = f = 35$. Notice that b, c, and d form a straight line: $b + c + d = 180$. Substitute the known values of c and d into this equation:

$$\begin{aligned} b + 35 + 80 &= 180 \\ b + 115 &= 180 \\ b &= 65 \end{aligned}$$

5. **40°:** If $c + g = 140$, then $i = 40$, because there are $180°$ in a triangle. Since k is vertical to i, k is also equal to 40.

6. **90°:** If $g = 90$, then the other two angles in the triangle, c and i, sum to 90. Since a and k are vertical angles to c and i, they sum to 90 as well.

7. **150°:** Angles f and k are vertical to angles g and i. The latter two angles, then, must also sum to 150. Therefore, the third angle in the triangle must be $180 - 150$, so $c = 30$. Because $c + b = 180$, $30 + b = 180$, and $b = 150$.

Chapter 3 of Geometry

Polygons

In This Chapter...

Chapter 3
Polygons

A polygon is defined as a closed shape formed by line segments. The polygons tested on the GMAT include the following:

- Three-sided shapes (triangles)
- Four-sided shapes (quadrilaterals)
- Other polygons with n sides (where n is five or more)

This section will focus on polygons of four or more sides. In particular, the GMAT emphasizes quadrilaterals—or four-sided polygons—such as squares, rectangles, and less common shapes including trapezoids and parallelograms.

Polygons are two-dimensional shapes—they lie in a plane. The GMAT tests your ability to work with different measurements associated with polygons. In this book, you will learn how to work with angles, lengths, perimeter, and area.

The GMAT also tests your knowledge of three-dimensional shapes formed from polygons, particularly rectangular solids and cubes. You will learn how to calculate surface area and volume.

Quadrilaterals: An Overview

The most common polygon tested on the GMAT, aside from the triangle, is the quadrilateral (any four-sided polygon). Almost all GMAT polygon problems involve the special types of quadrilaterals shown below:

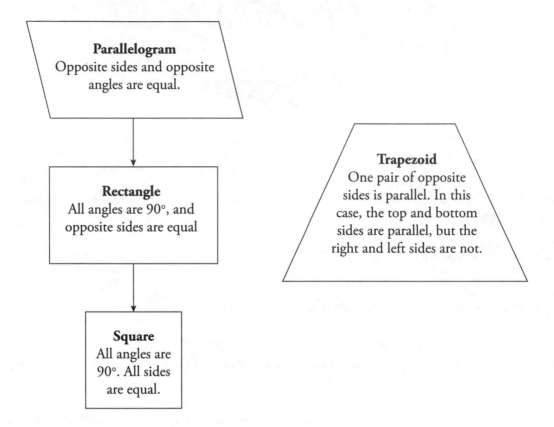

Parallelogram
Opposite sides and opposite angles are equal.

Rectangle
All angles are 90°, and opposite sides are equal

Square
All angles are 90°. All sides are equal.

Trapezoid
One pair of opposite sides is parallel. In this case, the top and bottom sides are parallel, but the right and left sides are not.

Polygons and Interior Angles

The sum of the interior angles of a given polygon depends only on the **number of sides in the polygon**. The following table displays the relationship between the type of polygon and the sum of its interior angles.

The sum of the interior angles of a polygon follows a specific pattern that depends on n, the number of sides that the polygon has.

Polygon	# of Sides	Sum of Interior Angles
Triangle	3	180°
Quadrilateral	4	360°
Pentagon	5	540°
Hexagon	6	720°

This pattern can be expressed with the following formula:

$(n - 2) \times 180$ = Sum of Interior Angles of a Polygon

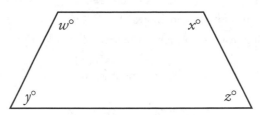

Since this polygon has four sides, the sum of its interior angles is $(4 - 2)180 = 2(180) = 360°$.

Alternatively, note that a quadrilateral can be cut into two triangles by a line connecting opposite corners. Thus, the sum of the angles is $2(180) = 360°$.

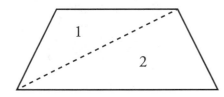

The interior angles of all four-sided polygons will always sum to 360°.

Since the next polygon shown to the right has six sides, the sum of its interior angles is $(6 - 2)180 = 4(180) = 720°$.

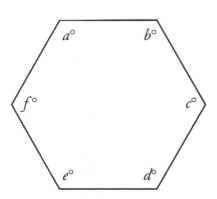

Alternatively, note that a hexagon can be cut into four triangles by three lines connecting corners:

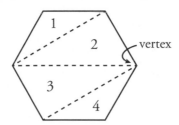

Thus, the sum of the angles is $4(180) = 720°$.

By the way, the corners of polygons are also known as vertices (singular: vertex).

Polygons and Perimeter

The perimeter refers to the distance around a polygon, or the sum of the lengths of all the sides. The amount of fencing needed to surround a yard would be equivalent to the perimeter of that yard (the sum of all the sides).

The perimeter of the pentagon to the right is: $9 + 7 + 4 + 6 + 5 = 31$.

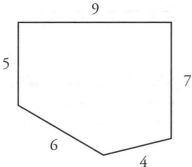

Polygons and Area

The area of a polygon refers to the space inside the polygon. Area is measured in square units, such as cm^2 (square centimeters), m^2 (square meters), or ft^2 (square feet). For example, the amount of space that a garden occupies is the area of that garden.

On the GMAT, you must know at least the first two area formulas:

1. Area of a Square = **Side** × **Side** = **Side²**

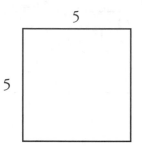

The side length of this square is 5. Therefore, the area is $5^2 = 25$.

2. Area of a Rectangle = **Length** × **Width**

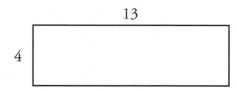

The length of this rectangle is 13, and the width is 4. Therefore, the area is $13 \times 4 = 52$.

The GMAT will occasionally ask you to find the area of a polygon more complex than a square or rectangle. The following formulas can be used to find the areas of other types of quadrilaterals:

3. Area of a Trapezoid = $\dfrac{(\textbf{Base}_1 + \textbf{Base}_2) \times \textbf{Height}}{2}$

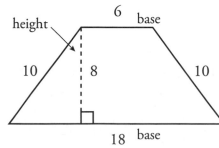

Note that the height refers to a line perpendicular to the two bases, which are parallel. (You often have to draw in the height, as in this case.) In the trapezoid shown, $base_1 = 18$, $base_2 = 6$, and the height = 8. The area is $(18 + 6) \times 8 \div 2 = 96$. Another way to think about this is to take the *average* of the two bases and multiply it by the height.

4. Area of any Parallelogram = **Base** × **Height**

Note that the height refers to the line perpendicular to the base. (As with the trapezoid, you often have to draw in the height.) In the parallelogram shown, the base is 5 and the height is 9. Therefore, the area is $5 \times 9 = 45$.

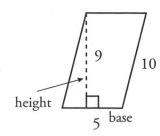

MANHATTAN
PREP

Note that some more complex shapes can be divided into a combination of rectangles and right triangles. For example:

Solving in this way will take longer than using the real formula, but trapezoids are infrequent enough that you might be willing to take that risk in order to avoid having to memorize yet another formula.

Three Dimensions: Surface Area

The GMAT tests two particular three-dimensional shapes formed from polygons: the rectangular solid and the cube.

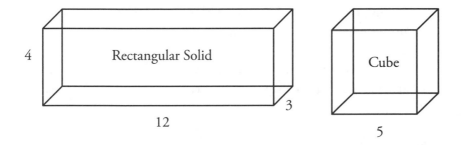

The surface area of a three-dimensional shape is the amount of space on the surface of that particular object. For example, the amount of paint that it would take to fully cover a rectangular box could be determined by finding the surface area of that box. As with simple area, surface area is measured in square units such as in² (square inches) or ft² (square feet).

Surface Area = the *sum* of *all* of the faces

Both a rectangular solid and a cube have **six faces**.

To determine the surface area of a rectangular solid, you must find the area of each face. Notice, however, that in a rectangular solid, the front and back faces have the same area, the top and bottom faces have the same area, and the two side faces have the same area. In the solid on the previous page, the area of the front face is equal to $12 \times 4 = 48$. Thus, the back face also has an area of 48. The area of the bottom face is equal to $12 \times 3 = 36$, so the top face also has an area of 36. Finally, each side face has an area of $3 \times 4 = 12$. Therefore, the surface area, or the sum of the areas of all six faces equals $48(2) + 36(2) + 12(2) = 192$.

To determine the surface area of a cube, you only need the length of one side. First, find the area of one face: $5 \times 5 = 25$. Then, multiply by six to account for all of the faces: $6 \times 25 = 150$.

Three Dimensions: Volume

The volume of a three-dimensional shape is the amount of "stuff" it can hold. "Capacity" is another word for volume. For example, the amount of liquid that a rectangular milk carton holds can be determined by finding the volume of the carton. Volume is measured in cubic units such as in³ (cubic inches), ft³ (cubic feet), or m³ (cubic meters).

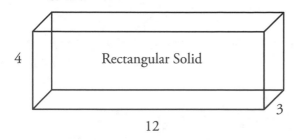
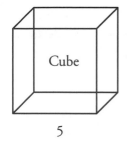

Volume = Length × Width × Height

The length of the rectangular solid above is 12, the width is 3, and the height is 4. Therefore, the volume is $12 \times 3 \times 4 = 144$.

In a cube, all three of the dimensions—length, width, and height—are identical. Therefore, knowing the measurement of just one side of the cube is sufficient to find the volume. In the cube above, the volume is $5 \times 5 \times 5 = 125$.

Beware of a GMAT volume trick, as in this example:

> How many books, each with a volume of 100 in³, can be packed into a crate with a volume of 5,000 in³?

It is tempting to answer "50 books" (since $50 \times 100 = 5,000$). However, this is incorrect, because you do not know the exact dimensions of each book! One book might be $5 \times 5 \times 4$, while another book might be $20 \times 5 \times 1$. Even though both have a volume of 100 in³, they have different rectangular shapes. Without knowing the exact shapes of all the books, you cannot tell whether they would all fit into the crate or whether there would be empty space because the 50 books don't fill the crate perfectly. Remember, when you are fitting three-dimensional objects into other three-dimensional objects, knowing the respective volumes is not enough. You must know the specific dimensions (length, width, and height) of each object to determine whether the objects can fit without leaving gaps.

Problem Set

Note: Figures are not drawn to scale.

1. 40 percent of Andrea's living room floor is covered by a carpet that is 4 feet by 9 feet. What is the area of her living room floor?

2. A pentagon has three sides with length x, and two sides with the length $3x$. If x is $\frac{2}{3}$ of an inch, what is the perimeter of the pentagon?

3. *ABCD* is a quadrilateral, with *AB* parallel to *CD* (see figure). Point *E* is between *C* and *D* such that *AE* represents the height of *ABCD*, and *E* is the midpoint of *CD*. If *AB* is 4 inches long, *AE* is 5 inches long, and the area of triangle *AED* is 12.5 square inches, what is the area of *ABCD*? (Note: figure not drawn to scale.)

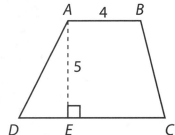

4. A rectangular swimming pool has a length of 30 meters, a width of 10 meters, and an average depth of 2 meters. If a hose can fill the pool at a rate of 0.5 cubic meters per minute, how many hours will it take the hose to fill the pool?

5. A rectangular solid has a square base, with each side of the base measuring 4 meters. If the volume of the solid is 112 cubic meters, what is the surface area of the solid?

Save the problem set below for review, either after you finish this book or after you finish all of the Quant books that you plan to study.

6. Frank the Fencemaker needs to fence in a rectangular yard. He fences in three of the four sides of the yard. The unfenced side of the yard is 40 feet long. The yard has an area of 280 square feet. What is the length, in feet, of the fence that Frank installs?

7. If the perimeter of a rectangular flower bed is 30 feet, and its area is 44 square feet, what is the length of each of its shorter sides?

8. A rectangular tank needs to be coated with insulation. The tank has dimensions of 4 feet, 5 feet, and 2.5 feet. Each square foot of insulation costs $20. How much will it cost to cover the surface of the tank with insulation?

9. There is a rectangular parking lot with a length of $2x$ and a width of x. What is the ratio of the perimeter of the parking lot to the area of the parking lot, in terms of x?

10. *ABCD* is a square picture frame (see figure). *EFGH* is a square inscribed within *ABCD* as a space for a picture. The area of *EFGH* (for the picture) is equal to the area of the picture frame (the area of *ABCD* minus the area of *EFGH*). If *AB* = 6, what is the length of *EF*?

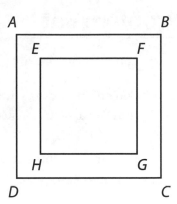

3

Solutions

1. **90 ft²:** The area of the carpet is equal to $l \times w$, or $4 \times 9 = 36$ ft². Set up a proportion to find the area of the whole living room floor:

$$\frac{40}{100} = \frac{36}{x}$$ Cross-multiply to solve.

$$40x = 3,600$$

$$x = 90 \text{ ft}^2$$

2. **6 inches:** The perimeter of a pentagon is the sum of its five sides: $x + x + x + 3x + 3x = 9x$. If x is $\frac{2}{3}$ of an inch, the perimeter is $9\left(\frac{2}{3}\right)$, or 6 inches.

3. **35 in²:** If E is the midpoint of C, then $CE = DE = x$. You can determine the length of x by using what you know about the area of triangle AED:

$$A = \frac{b \times h}{2}$$

$$12.5 = \frac{5x}{2}$$

$$25 = 5x$$

$$x = 5$$ Therefore, the length of CD is $2x$, or 10.

To find the area of the trapezoid, use the formula:

$$A = \frac{b_1 + b_2}{2} \times h$$

$$= \frac{4 + 10}{2} \times 5$$

$$= 35 \text{ in}^2$$

4. **20 hours:** The volume of the pool is (length) × (width) × (height), or $30 \times 10 \times 2 = 600$ cubic meters. Use a standard work equation, $RT = W$, where W represents the total work of 600 m³:

$$0.5t = 600$$

$$t = 1,200 \text{ minutes}$$

Convert this time to hours by dividing by 60: $1,200 \div 60 = 20$ hours.

Alternatively, you could convert first: $\frac{0.5\text{m}^3}{\text{min}} \times \frac{60\,\text{min}}{\text{hr}} = \frac{30\text{m}^3}{\text{hr}}$ Next, use the standard work equation:

$$30t = 600$$

$$t = 20 \text{ hours}$$

5. **144 m²:** The volume of a rectangular solid equals (length) × (width) × (height). If you know that the length and width are both 4 meters long, you can substitute values into the formulas as shown:

$$112 = 4 \times 4 \times h$$
$$h = 7$$

To find the surface area of a rectangular solid, sum the individual areas of all six faces:

	Area of One Face		**Total Area of Two Identical Faces**
Top and Bottom:	$4 \times 4 = 16$	→	$2 \times 16 = 32$
Sides:	$4 \times 7 = 28$	→	$4 \times 28 = 112$
All 6 faces		→	$32 + 112 = 144$ m²

6. **54 feet:** You know that one side of the yard is 40 feet long; call this the length. You also know that the area of the yard is 280 square feet. In order to determine the perimeter, you must know the width of the yard:

$$A = l \times w$$
$$280 = 40w$$
$$w = 280 \div 40 = 7 \text{ feet}$$

Frank fences in the two 7-foot sides and one of the 40-foot sides. Thus, he needs 54 feet of fence: $40 + 7 + 7 = 54$.

7. **4 feet:** Set up equations to represent the area and perimeter of the flower bed:

$$A = l \times w \qquad\qquad\qquad P = 2(l + w)$$

Then, substitute the known values for the variables A and P:

$$44 = l \times w \qquad\qquad\qquad 30 = 2(l + w)$$

Solve the two equations using the substitution method:

$$l = \frac{44}{w}$$

$$30 = 2\left(\frac{44}{w} + w\right)$$

Multiply the entire equation by $\frac{w}{2}$.

$$15w = 44 + w^2$$

$$w^2 - 15w + 44 = 0$$

$$(w - 11)(w - 4) = 0$$

$$w = \{4, 11\}$$

Solving the quadratic equation yields two solutions: 4 and 11. Each represents a possible side length. Since you were asked to find the length of the shorter side, the answer is the smaller of the two possible values, 4.

Alternatively, you can arrive at the correct solution by picking numbers. What length and width add up to 15 (half of the perimeter) and multiply to produce 44 (the area)? Some experimentation will demonstrate that the longer side must be 11 and the shorter side must be 4.

8. **$1,700:** To find the surface area of a rectangular solid, sum the individual areas of all six faces:

	Area of One Face		Total Area of Two Identical Faces
Top and Bottom:	$5 \times 4 = 20$	→	$20 \times 2 = 40$
Side 1:	$5 \times 2.5 = 12.5$	→	$12.5 \times 2 = 25$
Side 2:	$4 \times 2.5 = 10$	→	$10 \times 2 = 20$
All 6 faces		→	$40 + 25 + 20 = 85$ ft^2

Thus, covering the entire tank will cost $85 \times \$20$ which equals $1,700.

9. $\dfrac{3}{x}$ or **3 : x:** If the length of the parking lot is $2x$ and the width is x, you can set up a fraction to represent the ratio of the perimeter to the area as follows:

$$\frac{\text{perimeter}}{\text{area}} = \frac{2(2x + x)}{(2x)(x)} = \frac{6x}{2x^2} = \frac{3}{x}$$

10. $3\sqrt{2}$: The area of the frame and the area of the picture sum to the total area of the image, which is 6^2, or 36. Therefore, the area of the frame and the picture are each equal to half of 36, or 18. Since *EFGH* is a square, the length of *EF* is $\sqrt{18}$, or $3\sqrt{2}$.

Chapter 4 *of* Geometry

Triangles & Diagonals

In This Chapter...

Chapter 4
Triangles & Diagonals

The polygon most commonly tested on the GMAT is the triangle.

Right triangles (those with a 90° angle) require particular attention, because they have special properties that are useful for solving many GMAT Geometry problems.

The most important property of a right triangle is the unique relationship of the three sides. Given the lengths of any two of the sides of a right triangle, you can determine the length of the third side using the Pythagorean theorem. There are even two special types of right triangles—the 30–60–90 triangle and the 45–45–90 triangle—for which you only need the length of *one* side to determine the lengths of the other two sides.

Finally, right triangles are essential for solving problems involving other polygons. For instance, you might cut more complex polygons into right triangles.

The Angles of a Triangle

The angles in any given triangle have two key properties:

1. The sum of the three angles of a triangle equals 180°.

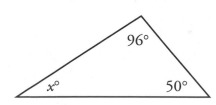

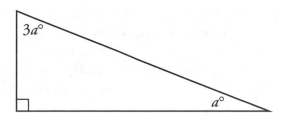

What is x? Since the sum of the three angles must be 180°, you can solve for x as follows:

$x = 180 - 96 - 50 = 34$

What is a? Since the sum of the three angles must be 180°, you can solve for x as follows:

$90 + 3a + a = 180 \rightarrow a = 22.5$.

2. Angles correspond to their opposite sides. This means that the largest angle is opposite the longest side, while the smallest angle is opposite the shortest side. Additionally, **if two sides are equal, their opposite angles are also equal.**

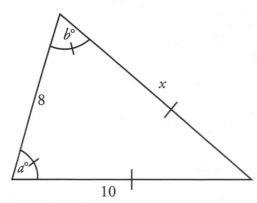

If $a = b$, what is the length of side x?

Since the side opposite angle b has a length of 10, the side opposite angle a must have the same length. Therefore, x is equal to 10.

Mark equal angles and equal sides with a slash, as shown. Also don't hesitate to redraw; if a figure doesn't match the dimensions you were given, redraw the triangle closer to scale.

The Sides of a Triangle

Consider the following "impossible" triangle *ABC* and what it reveals about the relationship between the three sides of any triangle.

The triangle to the right could never be drawn with the given measurements. Why? Consider that the shortest distance between any two points is a straight line. According to the triangle shown, the direct straight line distance between point *C* and point *B* is 14; however, the indirect path from point *C* to *B* (the path that goes from *C* to *A* to *B*) is 10 + 3, or 13, which is shorter than the direct path! This is impossible.

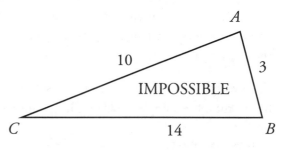

The example above leads to the following Triangle Inequality Law:

The sum of any two sides of a triangle must be *greater than* the third side.

Therefore, the maximum integer distance for side *BC* in the triangle above is 12. If the length of side *BC* is not restricted to integers, then this length has to be *less than* 13.

Note that the length cannot be smaller than a certain length, either. It must be *greater than* the difference between the lengths of the other two sides. In this case, side *BC* must be longer than 10 − 3, or 7. This is a consequence of the same idea.

Consider the following triangle and the proof that the given measurements are possible:

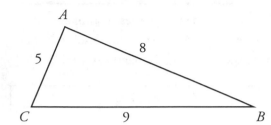

Test each combination of sides to prove that the measurements of this triangle are possible.

$8 + 5 > 9$	$8 - 5 < 9$
$9 + 5 > 8$	$9 - 5 < 8$
$9 + 8 > 5$	$9 - 8 < 5$

Note that the sum of two sides cannot be equal to the third side. The sum of two sides must always be **greater than** the third side. Likewise, the difference cannot be equal to the third side. The difference between two sides must be **less than** the third side.

If you are given two sides of a triangle, the length of the third side must lie between the difference and the sum of the two given sides. For instance, if you are told that two sides are of length 3 and 4, then the length of the third side must be between $4 - 3 = 1$ and $4 + 3 = 7$.

The Pythagorean Theorem

A right triangle is a triangle with one right angle (90°). Every right triangle is composed of two **legs** and a **hypotenuse**. The hypotenuse is the side opposite the largest angle (in this case, the right angle) and is often assigned the letter c. The two legs that form the right angle are often called a and b (it does not matter which leg is a and which leg is b).

Given the lengths of two sides of a right triangle, how can you determine the length of the third side? Use the Pythagorean theorem:

$$a^2 + b^2 = c^2$$

What is x?

$a^2 + b^2 = c^2$
$x^2 + 6^2 = 10^2$
$x^2 + 36 = 100$
$x^2 = 64$
$x = 8$

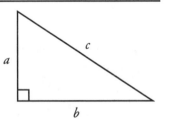

What is w?

$a^2 + b^2 = c^2$
$5^2 + 12^2 = w^2$
$25 + 144 = w^2$
$169 = w^2$
$13 = w$

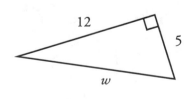

Common Right Triangles

Certain right triangles appear over and over on the GMAT. It pays to memorize these common combinations in order to save time on the exam. Instead of using the Pythagorean theorem to solve for the lengths of the sides of these common right triangles, memorize the following Pythagorean triples:

Common Combinations	Key Multiples
3–4–5	6–8–10
The most popular of all right triangles	9–12–15
$3^2 + 4^2 = 5^2$ $(9 + 16 = 25)$	12–16–20
5–12–13	
Also quite popular on the GMAT	10–24–26
$5^2 + 12^2 = 13^2$ $(25 + 144 = 169)$	
8–15–17	
This one appears less frequently.	None
$8^2 + 15^2 = 17^2$ $(64 + 225 = 289)$	

Watch out for impostor triangles! A non-right triangle with one side equal to 3 and another side equal to 4 does not have a third side of length 5.

Isosceles Triangles and the 45–45–90 Triangle

An isosceles triangle is one in which two of the three sides are equal. The two angles opposite those two sides will also be equal. The most important isosceles triangle on the GMAT is the isosceles right triangle.

An isosceles right triangle has one 90° angle (opposite the hypotenuse) and two 45° angles (opposite the two equal legs). This triangle is called the 45–45–90 triangle.

The lengths of the legs of every 45–45–90 triangle have a set ratio; memorize this:

leg	leg	hypotenuse
45°	45°	90°
x	x	$x\sqrt{2}$

Try an example:

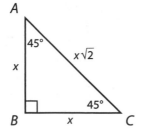

If the length of side *AB* is 5, what are the lengths of sides *BC* and *AC*?

MANHATTAN
PREP

The question tells you that AB is 5, so $x = 5$. Use the ratio $x : x : x\sqrt{2}$ for sides $AB : BC : AC$ to determine that the sides of the triangle have lengths $5 : 5 : 5\sqrt{2}$. Therefore, the length of side $BC = 5$ and the length of side $AC = 5\sqrt{2}$.

> For the same triangle, if the length of side AC is $\sqrt{18}$, what are the lengths of sides AB and BC?

Since the hypotenuse AC is $\sqrt{18}$:

$$x\sqrt{2} = \sqrt{18}$$
$$x = \frac{\sqrt{18}}{\sqrt{2}} = \sqrt{\frac{18}{2}}$$
$$x = \sqrt{9} = 3$$

Thus, the sides AB and BC are each equal to x, or 3.

Interestingly, the 45–45–90 triangle is exactly half of a square! That is, two 45–45–90 triangles put together make up a square. Thus, if you are given the diagonal of a square, you can use the 45–45–90 ratio to find the length of a side of the square.

4

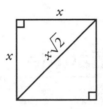

Equilateral Triangles and the 30–60–90 Triangle

An equilateral triangle is one in which all three sides (and all three angles) are equal. Each angle of an equilateral triangle is 60° (because all three angles must sum to 180°). A close relative of the equilateral triangle is the 30–60–90 triangle. Notice that two of these triangles, when put together, form an equilateral triangle:

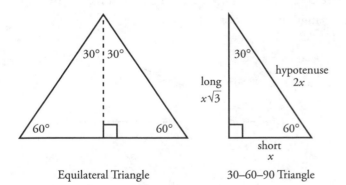

Equilateral Triangle

30–60–90 Triangle

The lengths of the legs of every 30–60–90 triangle have a set ratio; memorize this:

leg 30°	leg 60°	hypotenuse 90°
x	$x\sqrt{3}$	$2x$

Try some examples:

> If the short leg of a 30–60–90 triangle has a length of 6, what are the lengths of the long leg and the hypotenuse?

The question tells you that the short leg, which is opposite the 30° angle, is 6. Use the ratio $x : x\sqrt{3} : 2x$ to determine that the sides of the triangle have lengths $6 : 6\sqrt{3} : 12$. The long leg measures $6\sqrt{3}$ and the hypotenuse measures 12.

> If an equilateral triangle has a side of length 10, what is its height?

The side of an equilateral triangle is the hypotenuse of a 30–60–90 triangle created when the height of the equilateral triangle is drawn. Additionally, the height of an equilateral triangle is the same as the long leg of a 30–60–90 triangle. Since you are told that the hypotenuse is 10, use the ratio $x : x\sqrt{3} : 2x$ to set $2x = 10$ and determine that the multiplier x is 5. Therefore, the sides of the 30–60–90 triangle have lengths $5 : 5\sqrt{3} : 10$. The long leg has a length of $5\sqrt{3}$, which is the height of the equilateral triangle.

If you get tangled up on a 30–60–90 triangle, try to find the length of the short leg. The other legs will then be easier to figure out.

Exterior Angles of a Triangle

An **exterior angle** of a triangle is equal in measure to the sum of the two non-adjacent (opposite) **interior angles** of the triangle. For example:

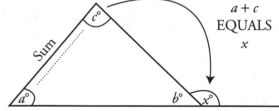

$a + b + c = 180$ (sum of angles in a triangle).
$b + x = 180$ (form a straight line).
Therefore, $x = a + c$.

In particular, look for exterior angles within more complicated figures. You might even redraw the figure with certain lines removed to isolate the triangle and exterior angle you need:

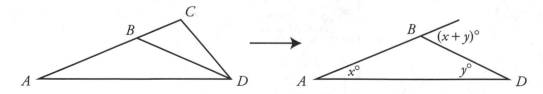

Triangles and Area

$$\text{Area of a Triangle} = \frac{\textbf{Base} \times \textbf{Height}}{\textbf{2}}$$

The base refers to the bottom side of the triangle. The height *always* refers to a line drawn from the opposite vertex to the base, creating a 90° angle.

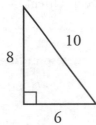

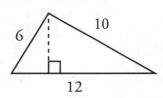

In the triangle on the left, the base is 6 and the height (perpendicular to the base) is 8. Therefore, the area is $(6 \times 8) \div 2 = 48 \div 2 = 24$.

In this triangle, the base is 12, but the height is not shown. Neither of the other two sides of the triangle is perpendicular to the base. In order to find the area of this triangle, you would first need to determine the height, which is represented by the dotted line.

Although you may commonly think of "the base" of a triangle as whichever side is drawn horizontally, you can designate any side of a triangle as the base. For example, the following three figures show the same triangle, with each side in turn designated as the base:

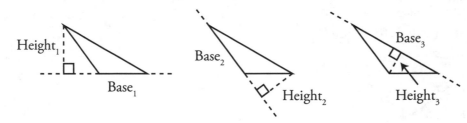

Since a triangle has only one area, the area must be the same regardless of the side chosen as the base. You can choose any pair of height and base that you like, as long as the height is a perpendicular line drawn from the opposite vertex to the base that you've chosen.

Right triangles have three possible bases just as other triangles do, but they are special because their two legs are perpendicular. Therefore, if one of the legs is chosen as the base, then the other leg is the height. Of course, you can also choose the hypotenuse as the base.

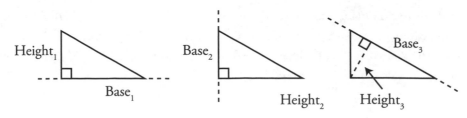

Thus, the area of a right triangle is given by the following formulas:

$$A = \frac{1}{2} \times \text{(One leg)} \times \text{(Other leg)} = \frac{1}{2} \text{(Hypotenuse)} \times \text{(Height from hypotenuse)}$$

Similar Triangles

One final tool that you can use for GMAT triangle problems is the similar triangle strategy. Often, looking for similar triangles can help you solve complex problems.

Triangles are defined as similar if all of their **corresponding angles are equal** and their **corresponding sides are in proportion**, as in the triangles below:

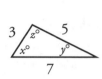 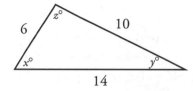

Once you find that two triangles have two pairs of equal (or congruent) angles, you know that the triangles are similar. If two sets of angles are congruent, then the third set of angles must be congruent, since the sum of the angles in any triangle is 180°.

Try an example:

What is the length of side *EF*?

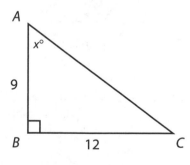 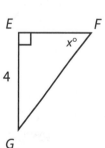

The two triangles above are similar because they have two angles in common (*x* and the right angle). Since they are similar triangles, their corresponding sides must be in proportion.

Side *BC* corresponds to side *EG* (since they both are opposite angle *x*). Because these sides are in the ratio of 12 : 4, you can determine that the large triangle is three times bigger than the smaller one. That is, the triangles are in the ratio of 3 : 1. Since side *AB* corresponds to side *EF*, and *AB* has a length of 9, you can conclude that side *EF* has a length of 3.

Problem Set

Note: Figures are not drawn to scale.

1. Two sides of a triangle have lengths 4 and 10. If the third side has a length of integer x, how many possible values are there for x?

2. In triangle ABC, $AD = DB = DC$ (see figure). If angle DCB is 60° and angle ACD is 20°, what is the value of x?

3. Beginning in Town A, Biker Bob rides his bike 10 miles west, 3 miles north, 5 miles east, and then 9 miles north, to Town B. How far apart are Town A and Town B? (Assume perfectly flat terrain.)

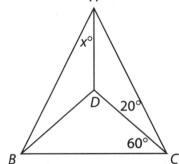

4. A square is bisected into two equal triangles (see figure). If the length of BD is $16\sqrt{2}$ inches, what is the area of the square?

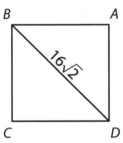

Save the problem set below for review, either after you finish this book or after you finish all of the Quant books that you plan to study.

5. What is the value of x in the figure to the right?

6. The size of a square computer screen is measured by the length of its diagonal. How much bigger is the visible area of a square 24-inch screen than the area of a square 20-inch screen?

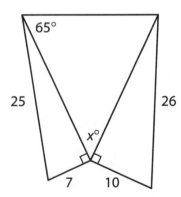

Solutions

1. **Seven:** If two sides of a triangle are 4 and 10, the third side must be greater than $10 - 4$ and smaller than $10 + 4$. Therefore, the possible values for x are {7, 8, 9, 10, 11, 12, and 13}. You can draw a sketch to convince yourself of this result:

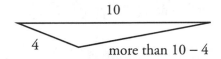 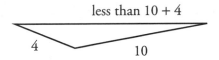

2. **10°:** If $AD = DB = DC$, then the three triangular regions in this figure are all isosceles triangles. Therefore, you can fill in some of the missing angle measurements as shown to the right. Since you know that there are 180° in the large triangle ABC, you can write the following equation:

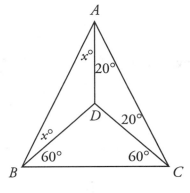

$$x + x + 20 + 20 + 60 + 60 = 180$$
$$2x + 160 = 180$$
$$x = 10$$

3. **13 miles:** If you draw a rough sketch of the path Biker Bob takes, as shown to the right, you can see that the direct distance from A to B forms the hypotenuse of a right triangle. The short leg (horizontal) is $10 - 5 = 5$ miles, and the long leg (vertical) is $9 + 3 = 12$ miles. Therefore, you can use the Pythagorean theorem to find the direct distance from A to B:

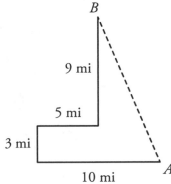

$$5^2 + 12^2 = c^2$$
$$25 + 144 = c^2$$
$$c^2 = 169 \qquad \text{You might recognize the common right triangle: 5–12–13. If so, you}$$
$$c = 13 \qquad \text{don't need to use the Pythagorean theorem to calculate the value of 13.}$$

4. **256 in²:** The diagonal of a square is $s\sqrt{2}$ and the given length of the diagonal in the problem is $16\sqrt{2}$. therefore, the side length of square $ABCD$ is $s = 16$ inches. The area of the square is s^2, or $16^2 = 256$.

5. **50°:** Use the Pythagorean theorem to establish the missing lengths of the two right triangles on the right and left sides of the figure:

$$7^2 + b^2 = 25^2 \qquad\qquad 10^2 + b^2 = 26^2$$
$$49 + b^2 = 625 \qquad\qquad 100 + b^2 = 676$$
$$b^2 = 576 \qquad\qquad\qquad b^2 = 576$$
$$b = 24 \qquad\qquad\qquad\quad b = 24$$

Alternatively, if you have the common right triangles memorized, notice that the second triangle (10–x–26) is the 5–12–13 triangle multiplied by 2. The missing length, therefore, is $12 \times 2 = 24$.

The inner triangle is isosceles. Therefore, both angles opposite the equal sides measure 65°. Since there are 180° in a right triangle, $x = 180 - 2(65) = 50$.

6. **88 in²:** If the diagonal of the larger screen is 24 inches, and it is always true for a square that $d = s\sqrt{2}$, then:

$$s = \frac{d}{\sqrt{2}} = \frac{24}{\sqrt{2}} = \frac{24(\sqrt{2})}{(\sqrt{2})(\sqrt{2})} = \frac{24\sqrt{2}}{2} = 12\sqrt{2}$$

By the same reasoning, the side length of the smaller screen is $\dfrac{20}{\sqrt{2}} = \dfrac{20(\sqrt{2})}{(\sqrt{2})(\sqrt{2})} = 10\sqrt{2}$.

The areas of the two screens are:

Large screen: $A = 12\sqrt{2} \times 12\sqrt{2} = 288$

Small screen: $A = 10\sqrt{2} \times 10\sqrt{2} = 200$

The visible area of the larger screen is 88 square inches bigger than the visible area of the smaller screen.

Chapter 5
of Geometry

Circles & Cylinders

In This Chapter...

Chapter 5

Circles & Cylinders

A circle is defined as the set of points in a plane that are equidistant from a fixed center point. A circle contains 360° (360 degrees).

Any line segment that connects the center point to a point on the circle is termed a **radius** of the circle. If point O is the center of the circle shown to the right, then segment OC is a radius.

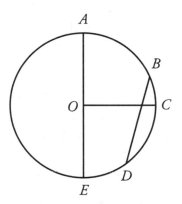

Any line segment that connects two points on a circle is called a **chord**. Any chord that passes through the center of the circle is called a **diameter**. Notice that the diameter is two times the length of the radius. Line segment BD is a chord of the circle shown to the right. Line segment AE is a diameter of the circle.

The GMAT tests your ability to find the circumference and the area of whole and partial circles. In addition, some advanced problems may test cylinders, which are three-dimensional shapes made, in part, of circles. The GMAT may test your ability to find the volume of cylinders.

Radius, Diameter, Circumference, and Area

The relationships between the radius, diameter, circumference, and area remain constant for every circle.

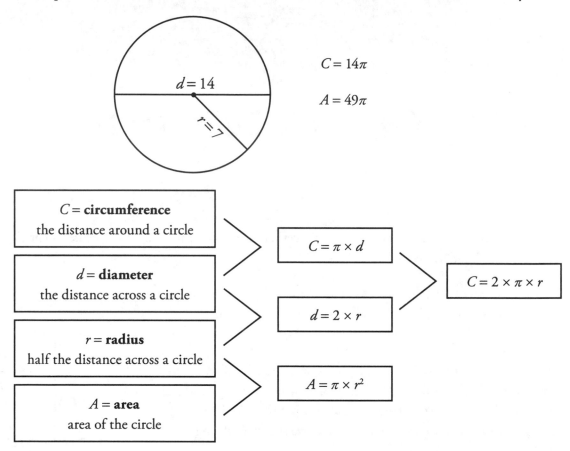

If you know *any* one of these values, you can determine the rest.

For Problem Solving questions, you will often need to use one of these values to solve for one of the other three. For Data Sufficiency questions, a little information goes a long way. If you know that you are able to solve for each of these values, you do not actually have to perform the calculation.

The space inside a circle is termed the area of the circle. This area is just like the area of a polygon. As with circumference, the only information you need to find the area of a circle is the radius of that circle. The formula for the area of any circle is:

$$A = \pi r^2$$

where A is the area, r is the radius, and π is a number that is approximately 3.14.

What is the area of a circle with a circumference of 16π?

In order to find the area of a circle, all you must know is its radius. If the circumference of the circle is 16π (and $C = 2\pi r$), then the radius must be 8. Plug this into the area formula:

$$A = \pi r^2 = \pi(8^2) = 64\pi$$

Area of a Sector

The GMAT may ask you to solve for the area of a sector of a circle, instead of the area of the entire circle. You can find the area of a sector by determining the fraction of the entire area that the sector occupies. Try an example:

> What is the area of sector *ACB* (the shaded region) below?

First, find the area of the entire circle:

$$A = \pi r^2 = \pi(3^2) = 9\pi$$

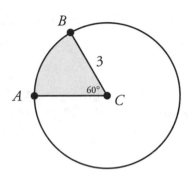

Then, use the central angle to determine what fraction of the entire circle is represented by the sector. Since the sector is defined by the central angle of 60°, and the entire circle is 360°, the sector occupies $\frac{60°}{360°}$, or one-sixth, of the area of the circle.

Therefore, the area of sector *ACB* is $\left(\frac{1}{6}\right)(9\pi) = 1.5\pi$.

Inscribed vs. Central Angles

Thus far, in dealing with arcs and sectors, you have learned about the **central angle**. A central angle is defined as an angle whose vertex lies at the center point of a circle. As discussed earlier, a central angle defines both an arc and a sector of a circle.

Another type of angle is termed an **inscribed angle**. An inscribed angle has its vertex on the circle itself. The following figures illustrate the difference between a central angle and an inscribed angle.

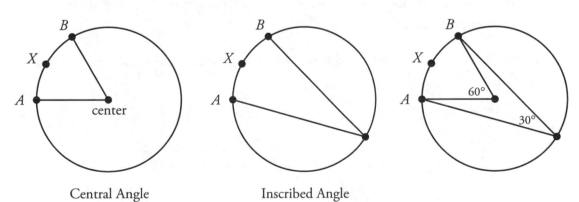

Central Angle   Inscribed Angle

Notice that, in the circle at the far right, there is a central angle and an inscribed angle, both of which intercept arc *AXB*. The arc is 60° (or one-sixth of the complete 360° circle). **An inscribed angle is equal to half of the arc it intercepts**, in degrees. In this case, the inscribed angle is 30°, which is half of 60°.

Inscribed Triangles

Related to this idea of an inscribed angle is that of an **inscribed triangle**. A triangle is said to be inscribed in a circle if all of the vertices of the triangle are points on the circle. The important rule to remember is: **if one of the sides of an inscribed triangle is a *diameter* of the circle, then the triangle *must* be a right triangle.** Conversely, any right triangle inscribed in a circle must have the diameter of the circle as one of its sides (thereby splitting the circle in half).

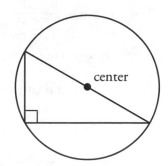

In the inscribed triangle to the right, triangle *ABC* must be a right triangle, since *AC* is a diameter of the circle.

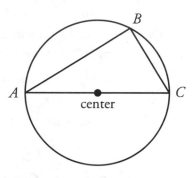

Cylinders and Volume

The volume of a cylinder measures how much "stuff" it can hold inside. In order to find the volume of a cylinder, use the following formula:

$$V = \pi r^2 h$$

V is the volume, *r* is the radius of the cylinder, and *h* is the height of the cylinder.

Determining the volume of a cylinder requires two pieces of information: (1) the radius of the cylinder and (2) the height of the cylinder.

The figures below show that two cylinders can have the same volume but different shapes (and therefore each fits differently inside a larger object):

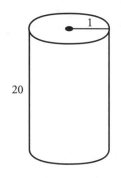

$$V = \pi r^2 h$$
$$= \pi(1)^2 20$$
$$= 20\pi$$

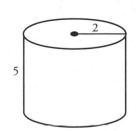

$$V = \pi r^2 h$$
$$= \pi(2)^2 5$$
$$= 20\pi$$

MANHATTAN
PREP

Problem Set

Note: Figures are not drawn to scale.

1. A circular lawn with a radius of 5 meters is surrounded by a circular walkway that is 4 meters wide (see figure). What is the area of the walkway?

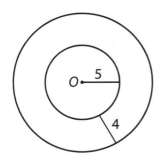

2. Randy can run π meters every 2 seconds. If the circular track has a radius of 75 meters, how many minutes does it take Randy to run twice around the track?

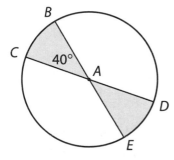

3. *BE* and *CD* are both diameters of circle with center A (see figure). If the area of the circle is 180 units², what is the total area of the shaded regions?

4. A cylindrical water tank has a diameter of 14 meters and a height of 20 meters. A water truck can fill π cubic meters of the tank every minute. How long will it take the water truck to fill the water tank from empty to half full?

5. A Hydrogenator water gun has a cylindrical water tank, which is 30 centimeters long. Using a hose, Jack fills his Hydrogenator with π cubic centimeters of his water tank every second. If it takes him 8 minutes to fill the tank with water, what is the diameter of the circular base of the gun's water tank?

Solutions

1. **$56\pi\,\text{m}^2$:** The area of the walkway is the area of the entire image (walkway + lawn) minus the area of the lawn. To find the area of each circle, use the formula:

Large circle: $A = \pi r^2 = \pi(9)^2 = 81\pi$

Small circle: $A = \pi r^2 = \pi(5)^2 = 25\pi$ Thus, $81\pi - 25\pi = 56\pi$ m².

2. **10 minutes:** The distance around the track is the circumference of the circle:

$$C = 2\pi r$$
$$= 150\pi$$

Running twice around the circle would equal a distance of 300π meters. If Randy can run π meters every 2 seconds, he runs 30π meters every minute. Therefore, it will take him 10 minutes to run around the circular track twice.

3. **40 units²:** The two central angles of the shaded sectors include a total of 80°. Simplify the fraction to find out what fraction of the circle this represents:

$$\frac{80}{360} = \frac{2}{9} \qquad \frac{2}{9} \text{ of 180 units}^2 \text{ is 40 units}^2.$$

4. **490 minutes**, or **8 hours and 10 minutes:** First find the volume of the cylindrical tank:

$$V = \pi r^2 \times h$$
$$= \pi(7)^2 \times 20$$
$$= 980\pi$$

If the water truck can fill π cubic meters of the tank every minute, it will take 980 minutes to fill the tank completely; therefore, it will take $980 \div 2 = 490$ minutes to fill the tank halfway. This is equal to 8 hours and 10 minutes.

5. **8 cm:** In 8 minutes, or 480 seconds, $480\pi\,\text{cm}^3$ of water flows into the tank. Therefore, the volume of the tank is 480π. You are given a height of 30, so you can solve for the radius:

$$V = \pi r^2 \times h$$
$$480\pi = 30\pi r^2$$
$$r^2 = 16$$
$$r = 4$$

Therefore, the diameter of the tank's base is 8 centimeters.

Chapter 6
of Geometry

Coordinate Plane

In This Chapter...

Chapter 6
Coordinate Plane

The coordinate plane is formed by a horizontal axis or reference line (the **"x-axis"**) and a vertical axis (the **"y-axis"**), as shown here. These axes are each marked off like a number line, with both positive and negative numbers. The axes cross at right angles at the number zero on both axes.

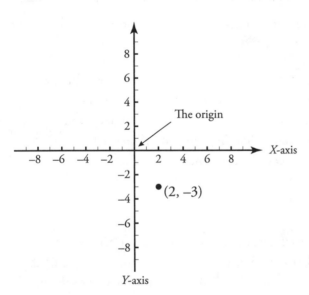

Points in the plane are identified by using an ordered pair of numbers, such as the point to the left, which is written as (2, −3). The first number in the ordered pair (2) is the **x-coordinate**, which corresponds to the point's horizontal location, as measured by the x-axis. The second number in the ordered pair (−3) is the **y-coordinate**, which corresponds to the point's vertical location, as indicated by the y-axis. The point (0, 0), where the axes cross, is called the **origin**.

A line in the plane is formed by the connection of two or more points. Notice that along the x-axis, the y-coordinate is 0. Likewise, along the y-axis, the x-coordinate is 0.

If the GMAT gives you coordinates with other variables, match them to x and y. For instance, if you have point (a, b), a is the x-coordinate and b is the y-coordinate.

Positive and Negative Quadrants

There are four quadrants in the coordinate plane, as shown in the figure below:

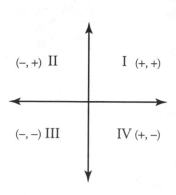

Quadrant I contains only those points with a **positive** *x*-coordinate and a **positive** *y*-coordinate.

Quadrant II contains only those points with a **negative** *x*-coordinate and a **positive** *y*-coordinate.

Quadrant III contains only those points with a **negative** *x*-coordinate and a **negative** *y*-coordinate.

Quadrant IV contains only those points with a **positive** *x*-coordinate and a **negative** *y*-coordinate.

The Slope of a Line

The slope of a line is defined as "rise over run"—that is, how much the line *rises* vertically divided by how much the line *runs* horizontally.

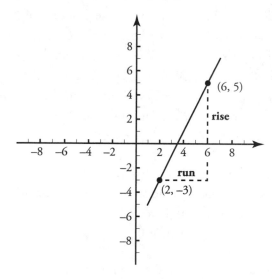

The slope of a line can be determined by taking any two points on the line and (1) determining the "rise," or difference between their *y*-coordinates, and (2) determining the "run," or difference between their *x*-coordinates. Thus:

$$\text{Slope} = \frac{\text{rise}}{\text{run}}$$

For example, in the graph on the left, the line rises vertically from −3 to +5. To find the distance, subtract the *y*-coordinates: $5 - (-3) = 8$. Thus, the line rises 8 units. The line also runs horizontally from 2 to 6. To find the distance, subtract the *x*-coordinates: $6 - 2 = 4$. Thus, the line runs 4 units.

Put the results together to find the slope of the line: $\dfrac{\text{rise}}{\text{run}} = \dfrac{8}{4} = 2$.

Two other points on the line may have a different rise and run, but the slope would be the same. The "rise over run" would always be 2 because a line has a constant slope.

The slope of a line is equal to $\dfrac{y_2 - y_1}{x_2 - x_1}$

For example, if you are given the two points (2, 3) and (4, −1), then the slope would be:

$$\frac{-1-3}{4-2} = \frac{-4}{2} = -2$$

You can choose to reorder the two points, but make sure that y_2 and x_2 always come from the same point (and that y_1 and x_1 always come from the same point). For example:

$$\frac{3-(-1)}{2-4} = \frac{4}{-2} = -2$$

Note that, either way, the slope is the same.

The Four Types of Slopes

A line can have one of four types of slopes:

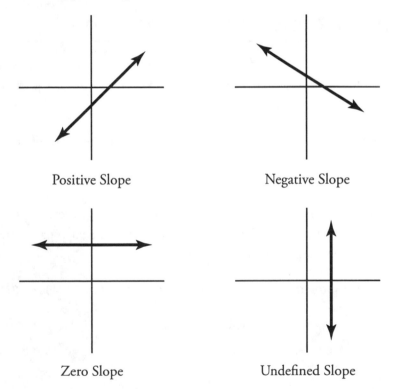

Positive Slope   Negative Slope

Zero Slope   Undefined Slope

A line with positive slope rises upward from left to right. A line with negative slope falls downward from left to right. A horizontal line has zero slope. A vertical line has undefined slope. Notice that the x-axis has zero slope, while the y-axis has undefined slope.

The Intercepts of a Line

A point where a line intersects a coordinate axis is called an **intercept**. There are two types of intercepts: the *x*-intercept, where the line intersects the *x*-axis, and the *y*-intercept, where the line intersects the *y*-axis.

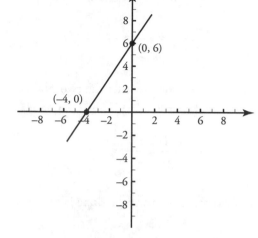

The *x*-intercept is expressed using the ordered pair $(x, 0)$, where *x* is the point where the line intersects the *x*-axis. **The *x*-intercept is the point on the line at which $y = 0$.** In this graph, the *x*-intercept is −4, as expressed by the ordered pair (−4, 0).

The *y*-intercept is expressed using the ordered pair $(0, y)$, where *y* is the point where the line intersects the *y*-axis. **The *y*-intercept is the point on the line at which $x = 0$.** In this graph, the *y*-intercept is 6, as expressed by the ordered pair (0, 6).

Slope-Intercept Equation: $y = mx + b$

Linear equations represent lines in the coordinate plane. Linear equations often look like this: $Ax + By = C$, where A, B, and C are numbers. For instance, $6x + 3y = 18$ is a linear equation. Linear equations never involve terms such as x^2, $\sqrt{x}$, or xy.

In coordinate plane problems, it is useful to write linear equations in the slope-intercept form:

$$y = mx + b$$

In this equation, *m* represents the slope of the line and *b* represents the *y*-intercept of the line, or the point at which the line crosses the *y*-axis. When you want to graph a linear equation, rewrite the equation in the slope-intercept form. Try this example:

> What is the slope-intercept form for a line with the equation $6x + 3y = 18$?

Rewrite the equation by solving for *y* as follows:

$$6x + 3y = 18$$
$$3y = 18 - 6x \qquad \text{Subtract } 6x \text{ from both sides}$$
$$y = 6 - 2x \qquad \text{Divide both sides by 3}$$
$$y = -2x + 6 \qquad \text{Thus, the } y\text{-intercept is } (0, 6), \text{ and the slope is } -2.$$

To graph this line, first put a point at +6 on the
y-axis (because the y-intercept, b, equals 6).

Then count down 2 units (because the slope is
negative) and to the right 1 unit. Place another point.

Draw a line between the two points.

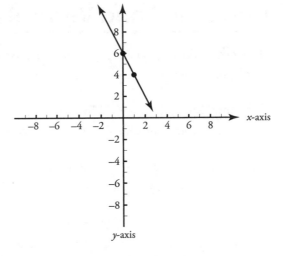

The GMAT sometimes asks you to determine which quadrants a given line passes through.
For example:

Which quadrants does the line $2x + y = 5$ pass through?

First, rewrite the line in the form $y = mx + b$:

$$2x + y = 5$$
$$y = 5 - 2x$$
$$y = -2x + 5$$

Next, sketch the line. Since $b = 5$, the y-intercept is the point $(0, 5)$. The

slope is -2, so the line slopes downward to the right from the y-intercept. A slope of -2 is the equiva-

lent of $\dfrac{-2}{1}$. Count one place to the right of the intercept (the run) and two places down (the "rise" of

a negative slope). Draw a second point, then connect the two points with a line. Although you do not
know exactly where the line intersects the x-axis, you can now see that the line passes through quadrants I, II, and IV.

Alternatively, find two points on the line by setting x and y equal to 0 in the original equation. In this
way, you find the x- and y-intercepts:

$$\begin{array}{ll}
x = 0 & y = 0 \\
2x + y = 5 & 2x + y = 5 \\
2(0) + y = 5 & 2x + (0) = 5 \\
y = 5 & x = 2.5
\end{array}$$

The points $(0, 5)$ and $(2.5, 0)$ are both on the line.

Now sketch the line, using the points you have identified. If you plot $(0, 5)$ and $(2.5, 0)$ on the coordinate plane, you can connect them to see the position of the line. Again, the line passes through quadrants I, II, and IV.

6

Horizontal and Vertical Lines

Horizontal and vertical lines are not expressed in the $y = mx + b$ form. Instead, they are expressed as simple, one-variable equations.

Horizontal lines are expressed in the form:
    $y = some$ $number$, such as $y = 2$ or $y = -7$

Vertical lines are expressed in the form:
    $x = some$ $number$, such as $x = 3$ or $x = 5$

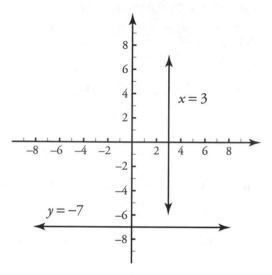

All the points on a vertical line have the same x-coordinate. This is why the equation of a vertical line is defined only by x. The y-axis itself corresponds to the equation $x = 0$. Likewise, all the points on a horizontal line have the same y-coordinate. This is why the equation of a horizontal line is defined only by y. The x-axis itself corresponds to the equation $y = 0$.

The Distance Between Two Points

The distance between any two points in the coordinate plane can be calculated by using the Pythagorean theorem. For example:

What is the distance between the points (1, 3) and (7, −5)?

Start by drawing a right triangle connecting the points, as shown.

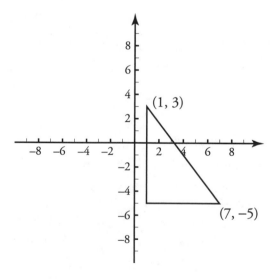

Next, find the lengths of the two legs of the triangle by calculating the rise and the run.

    The y-coordinate changes from 3 to −5, a difference of 8 (the vertical leg).

    The x-coordinate changes from 1 to 7, a difference of 6 (the horizontal leg).

MANHATTAN
PREP

Now, use the Pythagorean theorem to calculate the length of the diagonal, which is the distance between the points.

$$6^2 + 8^2 = c^2$$
$$36 + 64 = c^2$$
$$100 = c^2$$
$$c = 10$$

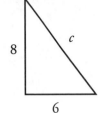

The distance between the two points is 10 units.

Alternatively, to find the hypotenuse, you might have recognized this triangle as a multiple of the 3–4–5 triangle (specifically, a 6–8–10 triangle).

6

Problem Set

1.   A line has the equation $y = 3x + 7$. At which point does this line intersect the y-axis?

2.   A line has the equation $x = -2y + z$. If (3, 2) is a point on the line, what is z?

3.   Which quadrants, if any, do NOT contain any points on the line represented by $x - y = 18$?

4.   A line has a slope of $\dfrac{1}{6}$ and intersects the x-axis at (−24, 0). At which point does this line intersect the y-axis?

Save the problem set below for review, either after you finish this book or after you finish all of the Quant books that you plan to study.

5.   A line has the equation $x = \dfrac{y}{80} - 20$. At which point does this line intersect the x-axis?

6.   Which quadrants, if any, do NOT contain any points on the line represented by $x = 10y$?

7.   Which quadrants, if any, contain points on the line represented by $x + 18 = 2y$?

8.   A line has a slope of $\dfrac{3}{4}$ and intersects the point (−12, −39). At which point does this line intersect the x-axis?

6

Solutions

1. **(0, 7):** A line intersects the y-axis at the y-intercept. Since this equation is written in slope-intercept form, the y-intercept is easy to identify: 7. Thus, the line intersects the y-axis at the point (0, 7).

2. **7:** Substitute the coordinates (3, 2) for x and y and solve for z:

$$3 = -2(2) + z$$
$$3 = -4 + z$$
$$z = 7$$

3. **II:** First, rewrite the line in slope-intercept form:

$$y = x - 18$$

Find the intercepts by setting x equal to 0 and y equal to 0:

$$y = 0 - 18 \qquad\qquad 0 = x - 18$$
$$y = -18 \qquad\qquad x = 18$$

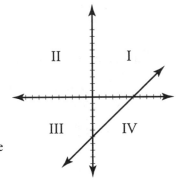

Plot the points: (0, −18), and (18, 0). From the sketch, you can see that the line does not pass through quadrant II.

4. **(0, 4):** Use the information given to find the equation of the line:

$$y = \frac{1}{6}x + b$$
$$0 = \frac{1}{6}(-24) + b$$
$$0 = -4 + b$$
$$b = 4$$

The variable b represents the y-intercept. Therefore, the line intersects the y-axis at (0, 4).

5. **(–20, 0):** A line intersects the x-axis at the x-intercept, or when the y-coordinate is equal to 0. Substitute 0 for y and solve for x:

$$x = 0 - 20$$
$$x = -20$$

6. **II and IV:** First, rewrite the line in slope-intercept form:

$$y = \frac{x}{10}$$

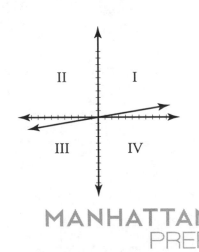

Notice from the equation that the y-intercept of the line is (0,0). This means that the line crosses the y-intercept at the origin, so the x- and *y*-intercepts are the same. To find another point on the line, substitute any convenient number for *x*; in this case, 10 would be a Smart Number to choose.

$$y = \frac{10}{10} = 1$$ The point (10, 1) is on the line.

Plot the points: (0, 0) and (10, 1). From the sketch, you can see that the line does not pass through quadrants II and IV.

7. **I, II, and III:** First, rewrite the line in slope-intercept form:

$$y = \frac{x}{2} + 9$$

Find the intercepts by setting *x* equal to 0 and *y* equal to 0:

$$0 = \frac{x}{2} + 9 \qquad\qquad y = \frac{0}{2} + 9$$
$$x = -18 \qquad\qquad y = 9$$

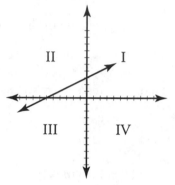

Plot the points: (−18, 0) and (0, 9). From the sketch, you can see that the line passes through quadrants I, II, and III.

8. **(40, 0):** Use the information given to find the equation of the line:

$$y = \frac{3}{4}x + b$$
$$-39 = \frac{3}{4}(-12) + b$$
$$-39 = -9 + b$$
$$b = -30$$

The line intersects the *x*-axis when *y* = 0. Set *y* equal to 0 and solve for *x*:

$$0 = \frac{3}{4}x - 30$$
$$\frac{3}{4}x = 30$$
$$x = 40$$

The line intersects the *x*-axis at (40, 0).

MANHATTAN
PREP

Chapter 7
of
Geometry

Extra Geometry

In This Chapter...

Chapter 7
Extra Geometry

Some difficult Geometry problems draw on the same geometric principles as easier problems. The GMAT makes these problems more difficult by adding steps. Other problems test more esoteric geometry rules, which you'll find in this chapter. For instance, to solve Problem Solving #145 in *The Official Guide for GMAT Quantitative Review 2015*, you have to complete several steps, using both Triangle concepts and Circle concepts. However, once you have labeled the figure appropriately, each step is itself straightforward. Likewise, Problem Solving #228 in *The Official Guide for GMAT Review 2015* does not contain fundamentally difficult Coordinate Plane Geometry. What makes #228 hard is its hybrid nature: it is a Combinatorics problem in a Coordinate Plane disguise.

The topics in this chapter rarely appear on the GMAT. If you want an exceptionally high Quant score, then study this chapter. Otherwise, you have our permission to skip this material and guess quickly if you do happen to get a problem testing one of these concepts on the real test.

Polygons and Area

Rarely, the GMAT might test someone on the area of a rhombus, so you should know the formula:

$$\text{Area of a rhombus} = \frac{\textbf{Diagonal}_1 \times \textbf{Diagonal}_2}{2}$$

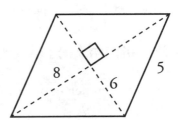

Note that the diagonals of a rhombus are *always* perpendicular bisectors (meaning that they cut each other in half at a 90° angle).

The area of the rhombus on the right is $\dfrac{6 \times 8}{2} = \dfrac{48}{2} = 24$.

Maximum Area of Polygons

In some problems, the GMAT may ask you to determine the maximum or minimum area of a given figure. This condition could be stated *explicitly*, as in Problem Solving questions ("What is the maximum area of … ?"), or *implicitly*, as in Data Sufficiency questions ("Is the area of rectangle *ABCD* less than 30?"). Following are two shortcuts that can help you optimize certain problems quickly.

Maximum Area of a Quadrilateral

Perhaps the most common maximum area problem is to maximize the area of a quadrilateral (usually a rectangle) with a *fixed perimeter*. If a quadrilateral has a fixed perimeter, say, 36 inches, it can take a variety of shapes:

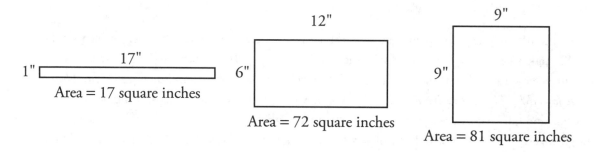

Of these figures, the one with the largest area is the square. This is a general rule: **of all quadrilaterals with a given perimeter, the *square* has the largest area**. This is true even in cases involving non-integer lengths. For instance, of all quadrilaterals with a perimeter of 25 feet, the one with the largest area is a square with $\frac{25}{4} = 6.25$ feet per side.

This principle can also be turned around to yield the following corollary: **of all quadrilaterals with a given area, the square has the minimum *perimeter*.**

Both of these principles can be generalized for *n* sides: a regular polygon with all sides equal will maximize area for a given perimeter and minimize perimeter for a given area.

Maximum Area of a Parallelogram or Triangle

Another common optimization problem involves maximizing the area of a *triangle or parallelogram with given side lengths*.

For instance, there are many triangles with two sides 3 and 4 units long. Imagine that the two sides of length 3 and 4 are on a hinge. The third side can have various lengths:

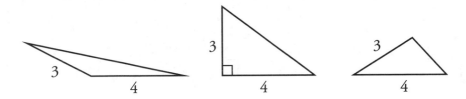

There are many corresponding parallelograms with two sides 3 and 4 units long:

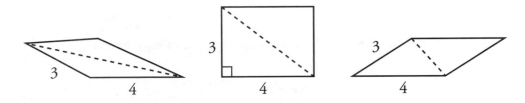

The area of a triangle is given by $A = \frac{1}{2}bh$ and the area of a parallelogram is given by $A = bh$. Because both of these formulas involve the perpendicular height h, the maximum area of each figure is achieved when the 3-unit side is perpendicular to the 4-unit side, so that the height is 3 units. All the other figures have lesser heights. (Note, that in this case, the triangle of maximum area is the famous 3–4–5 right triangle.) If the sides are not perpendicular, then the figure is squished, so to speak.

The general rule is this: **if you are given two sides of a triangle or parallelogram, you can maximize the area by placing those two sides *perpendicular* to each other.**

Since the rhombus is a special case of a parallelogram, this rule holds for rhombuses as well. All sides of a rhombus are equal. Thus, you can maximize the area of a rhombus with a given side length by making the rhombus into a square.

Triangles and Area

Because an **equilateral triangle** can be split into two 30–60–90 triangles, a useful formula can be derived for its area. If the side length of the equilateral triangle is S, then S is also the hypotenuse of each of the 30–60–90 triangles, so their sides are as shown in the figure below.

The equilateral triangle has base of length S and a height of length $\frac{S\sqrt{3}}{2}$.

Therefore, the **area of an equilateral triangle with a side of length S is**

equal to $\frac{1}{2}(S)\left(\frac{S\sqrt{3}}{2}\right) = \frac{S^2\sqrt{3}}{4}$.

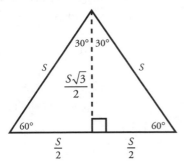

7

This formula can save you time, but it is not always needed on the test. If you find it easy to memorize formulas, then memorize this one. If you don't, then don't memorize it and take the risk that you won't see a problem like this on the test. If you do see one, you can always solve the long way.

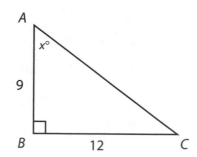

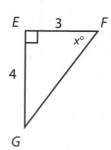

If you compute the areas of these two similar triangles, you get the following results:

$$\text{Area of } ABC = \frac{1}{2}bh \qquad\qquad \text{Area of } EFG = \frac{1}{2}bh$$

$$= \frac{1}{2}(9)(12) \qquad\qquad\qquad = \frac{1}{2}(3)(4)$$

$$= 54 \qquad\qquad\qquad\qquad = 6$$

These two areas are in the ratio of $54:6$, or $9:1$. Notice the connection between this $9:1$ ratio of the areas and the $3:1$ ratio of the side lengths. The $9:1$ ratio is the $3:1$ ratio *squared*.

This observation can be generalized:

> **If two similar triangles have corresponding side lengths in ratio $a:b$, then their areas will be in ratio $a^2:b^2$.**

The lengths being compared do not have to be sides—they can represent heights or perimeters. In fact, the figures do not have to be triangles. The principle holds true for *any* similar polygons, quadrilaterals, pentagons, etc.

Diagonals of Other Polygons

Right triangles are useful for more than just triangle problems. They are also helpful for finding the diagonals of other polygons, specifically squares, cubes, rectangles, and rectangular solids.

The diagonal of a square can be found using this formula:

$d = s\sqrt{2}$, where s is a side of the square.
This is also the face diagonal of a cube.

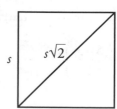

MANHATTAN
PREP

The main diagonal of a cube can be found using this formula:

$d = s\sqrt{3}$, where s is an edge of the cube.

Try an example:

> For a square with a side of length 5, what is the length of the diagonal?

To solve, plug 5 into the formula for a square, $d = s\sqrt{2}$. Thus, the length of the diagonal of the square is $5\sqrt{2}$.

> What is the measure of an edge of a cube with a main diagonal of length $\sqrt{60}$?

To solve, use the formula for a cube, $d = s\sqrt{3}$, and plug in the information you know as follows:

$$\sqrt{60} = s\sqrt{3} \rightarrow s = \frac{\sqrt{60}}{\sqrt{3}} = \sqrt{20}$$

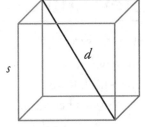

The length of the edge of the cube is $\sqrt{20}$.

To find the diagonal of a rectangle, you must know *either* the length and the width *or* one dimension and the proportion of one to the other. For example:

> If the rectangle to the right has a length of 12 and a width of 5, what is the length of the diagonal?

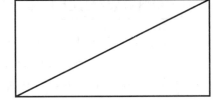

Using the Pythagorean theorem, solve:
$$5^2 + 12^2 = c^2 \rightarrow 25 + 144 = c^2 \rightarrow c = 13$$

The diagonal length is 13. Alternatively, note that this is a right triangle and you know two of the sides are 5 and 12. If you have memorized this common right triangle, then you know the length of the hypotenuse is 13. For example:

> If the rectangle above has a width of 6, and the ratio of the width to the length is 3:4, what is the diagonal?

Use the ratio to find the length: $\dfrac{3}{4} = \dfrac{6}{x}$. Therefore, $x = 8$. Then use the Pythagorean theorem or recognize that this is a 6–8–10 triangle. Either way, the diagonal length is 10.

> What is the length of the main diagonal of the rectangular solid in the figure to the right?

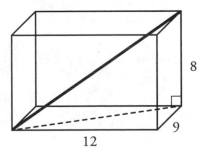

To find the diagonal of a rectangular solid, use the Pythagorean theorem twice.

First, find the diagonal of the bottom face: $9^2 + 12^2 = c^2$ yields $c = 15$ (this is a multiple of a 3–4–5 triangle), so the bottom (dashed) diagonal is 15. This bottom diagonal of length 15 is the base leg of another right triangle with a height of 8. Now use the Pythagorean theorem a second time: $8^2 + 15^2 = c^2$ yields $c = 17$, so the main diagonal is 17.

Alternatively, memorize the "Deluxe" Pythagorean theorem: $d^2 = x^2 + y^2 + z^2$, where x, y, and z are the sides of the rectangular solid and d is the main diagonal. In this case, $9^2 + 12^2 + 8^2 = d^2$, which yields $d = 17$.

Revolution = Circumference

The GMAT occasionally asks about a wheel or spinning circle. A full revolution, or turn, of a spinning wheel is equivalent to the wheel going around once. If you were to place a point on the edge of the wheel, it would travel one full circumference in one revolution. For example, if a wheel spins at 3 revolutions per second, a point on the edge travels a distance equal to 3 circumferences per second. If the wheel has a diameter of 4 feet, then the point travels at a rate of $3 \times 4\pi = 12\pi$ feet per second.

Circumference and Arc Length

Often, the GMAT will ask you to solve for a portion of the distance on a circle, instead of the entire circumference. This portion is termed an **arc**. Arc length can be found by determining what fraction the arc is of the entire circumference. For example:

In the circle to the right, what is the length of arc _AXB_?

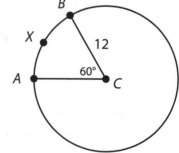

Arc _AXB_ is the arc from _A_ to _B_, passing through the point _X_. To find its length, first find the circumference of the circle. The radius is given as 12. To find the circumference, use the formula $C = 2\pi r$. Thus, $2\pi(12) = 24\pi$.

Next, use the central angle, the angle at the center of the circle when two lines are drawn to points _A_ and _B_, to determine what fraction the arc is of the entire circle. Since the arc is defined by the central angle of 60°, and the entire circle is 360°, then the arc is $\dfrac{60}{360} = \dfrac{1}{6}$ of the circle.

Therefore, the measure of arc _AXB_ is $\left(\dfrac{1}{6}\right)(24\pi) = 4\pi$.

Perimeter of a Sector

The boundaries of a **sector** of a circle are formed by the arc and two radii. Think of a sector as a slice of pizza. The arc corresponds to the crust, and the center of the circle corresponds to the tip of the slice.

If you know the length of the radius and the central angle, you can find the perimeter of the sector. For example:

> What is the perimeter of sector *ABC*?

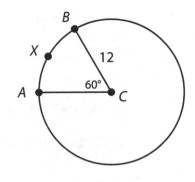

In the previous example, you found the length of arc *AXB*, which was 4π. Therefore, the perimeter of the sector is:

$$4\pi + 12 + 12 = 24 + 4\pi$$

Cylinders and Surface Area

Two circles and a rectangle combine to form a three-dimensional shape called a right circular cylinder (referred to from now on simply as a **cylinder**). The top and bottom of the cylinder are circles, while the middle of the cylinder is formed from a rolled-up rectangle, as shown in the figure below:

In order to determine the surface area (*SA*) of a cylinder, sum the areas of the three surfaces: the area of each circle is πr^2, while the area of the rectangle is length × width. The length of the rectangle is equal to the circumference of the circle ($2\pi r$), and the width of the rectangle is equal to the height of the cylinder (*h*). Therefore, the area of the rectangle is $2\pi r \times h$. To find the total surface area of a cylinder, add the area of the circular top and bottom, as well as the area of the rectangle that wraps around the outside.

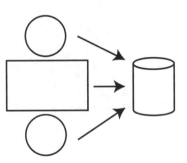

$$SA = \textbf{2 circles} + \textbf{rectangle} = 2(\pi r^2) + 2\pi rh$$

The only information you need to find the surface area of a cylinder is the radius of the cylinder and the height of the cylinder.

Step by Step: From Two Points to a Line

If you are given any two points on a line, you can write an equation for that line in the form $y = mx + b$. Here is an example showing the step-by-step method:

Find the equation of the line containing the points (5, –2) and (3, 4).

First, find the slope of the line by calculating the rise over the run.

The rise is the difference between the y-coordinates, while the run is the difference between the x-coordinates. The sign of each difference is important, so subtract the x-coordinates and the y-coordinates in the same order:

$$\frac{\text{rise}}{\text{run}} = \frac{y_1 - y_2}{x_1 - x_2} = \frac{-2-4}{5-3} = \frac{-6}{2} = -3 \qquad \text{The slope of the line is } -3.$$

Second, plug in the slope for m in the slope-intercept equation:

$y = -3x + b$

Third, solve for b, the y-intercept, by plugging the coordinates of one point into the equation. Either point's coordinates will work.

Plugging the point (3, 4) into the equation (3 for x and 4 for y) yields the following:

$4 = -3(3) + b$
$4 = -9 + b$
$b = 13$

The y-intercept of the line is 13.

Fourth, write the equation in the form $y = mx + b$:

$y = -3x + 13$ This is the equation of the line.

Note that sometimes the GMAT will only give you one point on the line, along with the y-intercept. This is the same thing as giving you two points on the line, because the y-intercept is a point! A y-intercept of 4 is the same as the ordered pair (0, 4).

Perpendicular Bisectors

The perpendicular bisector of a line segment forms a 90° angle with that line segment and divides the segment exactly in half. Questions about perpendicular bisectors are rare on the GMAT, but they do appear occasionally. For example:

> If the coordinates of point *A* are (2, 2) and the coordinates of point *B* are (0, –2), what is the equation of the perpendicular bisector of line segment *AB*?

The key to solving perpendicular bisector problems is to use this property: the perpendicular bisector has the **negative reciprocal slope** of the line segment it bisects. That is, the product of the two slopes is –1. (The only exception occurs when one line is horizontal and the other line is vertical, since vertical lines have undefined slopes.)

To start, find the slope of segment *AB*.

$$\text{slope} = \frac{\text{rise}}{\text{run}} = \frac{y_1 - y_2}{x_1 - x_2} = \frac{2 - (-2)}{2 - 0} = \frac{4}{2} = 2$$

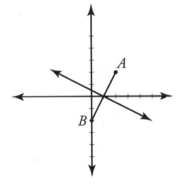

The slope of *AB* is 2.

Next, find the slope of the perpendicular bisector of *AB*.

Since perpendicular lines have negative reciprocal slopes, flip the fraction and change the sign to find the slope of the perpendicular bisector. The slope of *AB* is 2, or $\frac{2}{1}$. Therefore, the slope of the perpendicular bisector of *AB* is $-\frac{1}{2}$.

Now you know that the equation of the perpendicular bisector has the following form:

$$y = -\frac{1}{2}x + b$$

However, you still need to find the value of *b* (the *y*-intercept). To do this, you first need to find the point where the line bisects line segment *AB*. Then you plug the coordinates of this point into the equation above.

Now you can find the midpoint of *AB*.

The perpendicular bisector passes through the midpoint of *AB*. Thus, if you find the midpoint of *AB*, you will have found a point on the perpendicular bisector. Organize a table such as the one shown below to find the coordinates of the midpoint. Write the *x*- and *y*-coordinates of *A* and *B*. The coordinates of the midpoint will be the numbers halfway between each pair of *x*- and *y*-coordinates. In other

7

words, the *x*-coordinate of the midpoint is the *average* of the *x*-coordinates of *A* and *B*. Likewise, the *y*-coordinate of the midpoint is the *average* of the *y*-coordinates of *A* and *B*. This process will yield the midpoint of any line segment.

	x	*y*
A	2	2
Midpoint	**1**	**0**
B	0	−2

Finally, put the information together.

To find the value of *b* (the *y*-intercept), substitute the coordinates of the midpoint into the line equation for *x* and *y*:

$$0 = -\frac{1}{2}(1) + b$$

$$b = \frac{1}{2}$$

The perpendicular bisector of segment *AB* has the equation: $y = -\frac{1}{2}x + \frac{1}{2}$.

In summary, the following rules can be given:

- **Parallel lines have equal slopes: $m_1 = m_2$.**

- **Perpendicular lines have negative reciprocal slopes.** $\frac{-1}{m_1} = m_2$, **or** $m_1 \cdot m_2 = -1$.

- The **midpoint** between point $A(x_1, y_1)$ and point $B(x_2, y_2)$ is $\left(\frac{x_1 + x_2}{2}, \frac{y_1 + y_2}{2} \right)$.

The Intersection of Two Lines

Recall that a line in the coordinate plane is defined by a linear equation relating *x* and *y*. That is, if a point (*x*, *y*) lies on the line, then those values of *x* and *y* satisfy the equation. For instance, the point (3, 2) lies on the line defined by the equation *y* = 4*x* − 10, since the equation is true when you plug in *x* = 3 and *y* = 2:

$$y = 4x - 10$$
$$2 = 4(3) - 10 = 12 - 10$$
$$2 = 2 \quad \text{TRUE}$$

MANHATTAN
PREP

On the other hand, the point (7, 5) does not lie on that line, because the equation is false when you plug in $x = 7$ and $y = 5$:

$$y = 4x - 10$$
$$5 = 4(7) - 10 = 28 - 10$$
$$5 = 18 \quad \text{FALSE}$$

So what does it mean when two lines intersect in the coordinate plane? It means that at the point of intersection, *both* equations representing the lines are true. That is, the pair of numbers (x, y) that represents the point of intersection solves *both* equations. Finding this point of intersection is equivalent to solving a system of two linear equations. You can find the intersection by using algebra more easily than by graphing the two lines. Here's an example:

At what point does the line represented by $y = 4x - 10$ intersect the line represented by $2x + 3y = 26$?

Since $y = 4x - 10$, replace y in the second equation with $4x - 10$ and solve for x:

$$2x + 3(4x - 10) = 26$$
$$2x + 12x - 30 = 26$$
$$14x = 56$$
$$x = 4$$

Now solve for y. You can use either equation:

$$y = 4x - 10$$
$$y = 4(4) - 10$$
$$y = 16 - 10 = 6$$
$$y = 6$$

Thus, the point of intersection of the two lines is (4, 6).

If two lines in a plane do not intersect, then the lines are parallel. If this is the case, there is *no* pair of numbers (x, y) that satisfies both equations at the same time.

There is one other possibility: the two equations might represent the same line. In this case, infinitely many points (x, y) along the line satisfy the two equations (which must actually be the same equation in two different forms).

7

Function Graphs and Quadratics

You can think of the slope-intercept form of a linear equation as a function: $y = f(x) = mx + b$. That is, you input the x-coordinate into the function $f(x) = mx + b$, and the output is the y-coordinate of the point that you plot on the line.

You can apply this process more generally. For instance, imagine that $y = f(x) = x^2$. You can generate the graph for $f(x)$ by plugging in a variety of values for x and getting values for y. The points (x, y) that you find lie on the graph of $y = f(x) = x^2$.

x	$f(x) = y$	Point
−3	$(-3)^2 = 9$	(−3, 9)
−2	$(-2)^2 = 4$	(−2, 4)
−1	$(-1)^2 = 1$	(−1, 1)
0	$0^2 = 0$	(0, 0)
1	$1^2 = 1$	(1, 1)
2	$2^2 = 2$	(2, 4)
3	$3^2 = 9$	(3, 9)

This curved graph is called a **parabola**. Any function of the form $f(x) = ax^2 + bx + c$, where a, b, and c are constants, is called a **quadratic function** and can be plotted as a parabola in the coordinate plane. Depending on the value of a, the curve will have different shapes:

Positive value for a	Curve opens upward
Negative value for a	Curve opens downward
Large $|a|$ (absolute value)	Narrow curve
Small $|a|$	Wide curve

The parabola will always open upward or downward.

The most important questions you will be asked about the parabola are these:

  1. How many times does the parabola touch the x-axis?
  2. If the parabola does touch the x-axis, where does it touch?

In other words, how many x-intercepts are there and what are they?

These questions are important because the x-axis is the line representing $y = 0$. In other words, the parabola touches the x-axis at those values of x that make $f(x) = 0$. Therefore, these values solve the quadratic equation given by $f(x) = ax^2 + bx + c = 0$.

You can solve for 0 by factoring and solving the equation directly. Alternatively, you might plug in points and draw the parabola. Finally, for some very difficult problems, you could use the quadratic formula (though note that you will almost certainly never need to use this on the test, so this may not be worth memorizing):

$$x = \frac{-b \pm \sqrt{b^2 - 4ac}}{2a}$$

One solution is $\dfrac{-b + \sqrt{b^2 - 4ac}}{2a}$, and the other is $\dfrac{-b - \sqrt{b^2 - 4ac}}{2a}$.

The vast majority of GMAT Quadratic problems can be solved *without* using the quadratic formula. If you do apply this formula, the advantage is that you can quickly tell how many solutions the equation has by looking at just one part: the expression under the radical sign, $b^2 - 4ac$. This expression is known as the **discriminant,** because it discriminates or distinguishes three cases for the number of solutions to the equation, as follows:

1. If $b^2 - 4ac > 0$, then the square root operation yields a positive number. The quadratic formula produces *two roots* of the quadratic equation. This means that the parabola crosses the x-axis twice and has two x-intercepts.

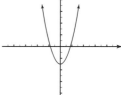

2. If $b^2 - 4ac = 0$, then the square root operation yields 0. The quadratic formula only produces *one root* of the quadratic equation. This means that the parabola touches the x-axis only once and has just one x-intercept.

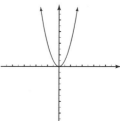

3. If $b^2 - 4ac < 0$ then the square root operation cannot be performed. This means that the quadratic formula produces *no roots* of the quadratic equation and the parabola never touches the x-axis (it has no x-intercepts).

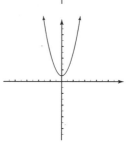

7

It is possible for the GMAT to ask you to graph other nonlinear functions of x. The following statements lie at the heart of all problems involving graphs of other nonlinear functions, as well as lines and parabolas:

1.   If a point lies on the graph, then you can plug its coordinates into the equation $y = f(x)$. Conversely, if a value of x and a value of y satisfy the equation $y = f(x)$, then the point (x, y) lies on the graph of $f(x)$.
2.   To find x-intercepts, find the values of x for which $y = f(x) = 0$.
3.   To find y-intercepts, set $x = 0$ and find $y = f(0)$.

Problem Set

1. What is the maximum possible area of a quadrilateral with a perimeter of 80 centimeters?

2. What is the minimum possible perimeter of a quadrilateral with an area of 1,600 square feet?

3. What is the maximum possible area of a parallelogram with one side of length 2 meters and a perimeter of 24 meters?

4. What is the maximum possible area of a triangle with a side of length 7 units and another side of length 8 units?

5. The lengths of the two shorter legs of a right triangle add up to 40 units. What is the maximum possible area of the triangle?

6. What is x in the figure below?

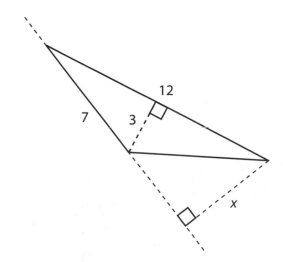

7. The line represented by the equation $y = -2x + 6$ is the perpendicular bisector of the line segment AB. If A has the coordinates $(7, 2)$, what are the coordinates for B?

8. How many x-intercepts does $f(x) = x^2 + 3x + 3$ have?

9. The line represented by the equation $y = x$ is the perpendicular bisector of line segment AB. If A has the coordinates $(-3, 3)$, what are the coordinates of B?

10. What are the coordinates for the point on line AB (see figure at right) that is three times as far from A as from B, and that is in between points A and B?

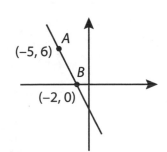

11. Triangle *A* has a base of *x* and a height of 2*x*. Triangle *B* is similar to triangle *A*, and has a base of 2*x*. What is the ratio of the area of triangle *A* to triangle *B*?

12. What is the longest diagonal of a rectangular box that is 120 inches long, 90 inches wide, and 80 inches tall?

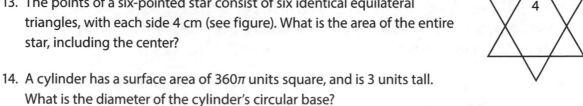

13. The points of a six-pointed star consist of six identical equilateral triangles, with each side 4 cm (see figure). What is the area of the entire star, including the center?

14. A cylinder has a surface area of 360π units square, and is 3 units tall. What is the diameter of the cylinder's circular base?

15. Angle *ABC* is 40° (see figure) and the area of the circle is 81π. If *CB* is a diameter of the circle, how long is arc *AXC*?

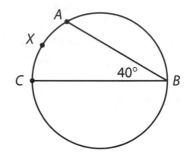

Solutions

1. **400 cm²:** The quadrilateral with maximum area for a given perimeter is a square, which has four equal sides. Therefore, the square that has a perimeter of 80 centimeters has sides of length 20 centimeters each. Since the area of a square is the side length squared, the area is: (20 cm)(20 cm) = 400 cm².

2. **160 ft:** The quadrilateral with minimum perimeter for a given area is a square. Since the area of a square is the side length squared, you can solve the equation $x^2 = 1,600$ ft² for the side length x, yielding $x = 40$ ft. The perimeter, which is four times the side length, is (4)(40 ft), which equals 160 ft.

3. **20 m²:** If one side of the parallelogram is 2 meters long, then the opposite side must also be 2 meters long. You can solve for the unknown sides, which are equal in length, by writing an equation for the perimeter: $24 = 2(2) + 2x$, with x as the unknown side. Solving, you get $x = 10$ meters. The parallelogram with these dimensions and maximum area is a *rectangle* with 2 meter and 10 meter sides. Thus, the maximum possible area of the figure is: (2 m)(10 m) = 20 m².

4. **28 square units:** A triangle with two given sides has maximum area if these two sides are placed at right angles to each other. For this triangle, one of the given sides can be considered the base, and the other side can be considered the height (because they meet at a right angle). Thus, plug these sides into the formula $A = \frac{1}{2}bh$: $A = \frac{1}{2}(7)(8) = 28$.

5. **200 square units:** You can think of a right triangle as half of a rectangle. Constructing this right triangle with legs adding to 40 is equivalent to constructing the rectangle with a perimeter of 80. Since the area of the triangle is half that of the rectangle, you can use the previously mentioned technique for maximizing the area of a rectangle: of all rectangles with a given perimeter, the *square* has the greatest area. The desired rectangle is thus a 20 by 20 square, and the right triangle has an area of $\left(\frac{1}{2}\right)(20)(20) = 200$ units.

6. $\frac{36}{7}$: You can calculate the area of the triangle using the side of length 12 as the base:

$$\left(\frac{1}{2}\right)(12)(3) = 18$$

Next, use the side of length 7 as the base and write the equation for the area:

$$\left(\frac{1}{2}\right)(7)(x) = 18$$

Now solve for x, the unknown height:

$$7x = 36$$
$$x = \frac{36}{7}$$

Alternatively, the large overall triangle is similar to the small triangle on the left side of the picture because they have the same angle measurements (both are right triangles, and they also share one angle in the far left tip of the figure). Draw these two triangles side by side and match up the sides. The hypotenuse of 7 in the smaller triangle "matches up" with the hypotenuse of 12 in the larger triangle, so the ratio of the two triangles is $\dfrac{12}{7}$. Multiply the known leg 3 in the smaller triangle by the ratio multiplier $\dfrac{12}{7}$ to get $3 \times \dfrac{12}{7} = \dfrac{36}{7}$. The value of x is $\dfrac{36}{7}$.

7. **(–1, –2):** If $y = -2x + 6$ is the perpendicular bisector of segment AB, then the line containing segment AB must have a slope of 0.5 (the negative inverse of –2). You can represent this line with the equation $y = 0.5x + b$. Substitute the coordinates (7, 2) into the equation to find the value of b.

	x	y
A	7	2
Midpoint	3	0
B	–1	–2

$$2 = 0.5(7) + b.$$
$$b = -1.5$$

The line containing AB is $y = 0.5x - 1.5$.

Find the point at which the perpendicular bisector intersects AB by setting the two equations, $y = -2x + 6$ and $y = 0.5x - 1.5$, equal to each other:

$$-2x + 6 = 0.5x - 1.5$$
$$2.5x = 7.5$$
$$x = 3; y = 0$$

The two lines intersect at (3, 0), which is the midpoint of AB.

Use a table to find the coordinates of B. The x- and y- coordinates of the midpoint are the averages of the x- and y- coordinates, respectively, of A and B.

8. **None:** There are three ways to solve this equation. The first is to attempt to factor the quadratic equation to find solutions. Since no two integers multiply to 3 and add to 3, this strategy fails.

The second approach is to pick numbers for x, solve for $f(x)$ (plotted as y in the coordinate plane), and plot these (x, y) pairs to determine the shape of the parabola. An example of this technique is displayed to the right.

x	$x^2 + 3x + 3 = y$	Point
–3	$9 - 9 + 3 = 3$	(–3, 3)
–2	$4 - 6 + 3 = 1$	(–2, 1)
–1	$1 - 3 + 3 = 1$	(–1, 1)
0	$0 + 0 + 3 = 3$	(0, 3)
1	$1 + 3 + 3 = 7$	(1, 7)

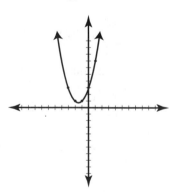

This approach demonstrates that the parabola never touches the x-axis. There are no x-intercepts.

The third method is to use the discriminant of the quadratic equation to count the number of x-intercepts.

First, identify the coefficients of each term. The function is $f(x) = x^2 + 3x + 3$. Matching this up to the definition of the standard quadratic equation, $f(x) = ax^2 + bx + c$, you have $a = 1$, $b = 3$, and $c = 3$.

Next, write the discriminant from the quadratic formula (the expression that is under the radical sign in the quadratic formula):

$$b^2 - 4ac = 3^2 - 4(1)(3)$$
$$= 9 - 12$$
$$= -3$$

Since the discriminant is less than 0, you cannot take its square root. This means that there is no solution to the equation $f(x) = x^2 + 3x + 3 = 0$, so the function's graph does not touch the x-axis. There are no x-intercepts.

9. **(3, −3):** Perpendicular lines have negative inverse slopes. Therefore, if $y = x$ is perpendicular to segment AB, you know that the slope of the perpendicular bisector is 1, and therefore the slope of segment AB is −1. The line containing segment AB takes the form of $y = -x + b$. To find the value of b, substitute the coordinates of A, (−3, 3), into the equation:

$$3 = -(-3) + b$$
$$b = 0$$

The line containing segment AB is $y = -x$.

Find the point at which the perpendicular bisector intersects AB by setting the two equations, $y = x$ and $y = -x$, equal to each other:

$$x = -x$$
$$x = 0;\ y = 0$$

The two lines intersect at (0, 0), which is the midpoint of AB. Use a table to find the coordinates of B.

10. **(−2.75, 1.5):** The point in question is 3 times farther from A than it is from B. You can represent this fact by labeling the point $3x$ units from A and x units from B as shown, giving a total distance of $4x$ between the two points. If you drop vertical lines from the point and from A to the x-axis, you get two similar triangles, the smaller of which is a quarter of the larger. (You can get this relationship from the fact that the larger triangle's hypotenuse is 4 times larger than the hypotenuse of the smaller triangle.)

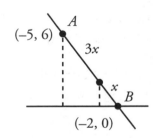

The horizontal distance between points A and B is 3 units (from −2 to −5). Therefore, $4x = 3$, so $x = 0.75$. The horizontal distance from B to the point is x, or 0.75 units. The x-coordinate of the point is 0.75 away from −2, or −2.75.

The vertical distance between points A and B is 6 units (from 0 to 6).

Therefore, $4x = 6$, so $x = 1.5$. The vertical distance from B to the point is x, or 1.5 units. The y-coordinate of the point is 1.5 away from 0, or 1.5.

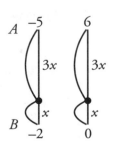

11. **1 to 4:** Since you know that triangle B is similar to triangle A, you can set up a proportion to represent the relationship between the sides of both triangles:

$$\frac{base}{height} = \frac{x}{2x} = \frac{2x}{?}$$

By proportional reasoning, the height of triangle B must be $4x$. Calculate the area of each triangle with the area formula:

Triangle A: $A = \dfrac{b \times h}{2} = \dfrac{(x)(2x)}{2} = x^2$

Triangle B: $A = \dfrac{b \times h}{2} = \dfrac{(2x)(4x)}{2} = 4x^2$

The ratio of the area of triangle A to triangle B is 1 to 4. Alternatively, you can simply square the base ratio of 1 : 2.

12. **170 inches:** Using the Deluxe Pythagorean theorem, calculate the length of the diagonal:

$$120^2 + 90^2 + 80^2 = d^2.$$

Note: to make the math easier, drop a 0 from each number—but don't forget to put it back in later!

$$12^2 + 9^2 + 8^2 = d^2$$
$$144 + 81 + 64 = d^2$$
$$289 = d^2$$
$$17 = d \qquad \textit{Don't forget to put the zero back in!}$$
$$d = 170 \text{ inches}$$

Alternatively, you can find the diagonal of this rectangular solid by applying the Pythagorean Theorem twice. First, find the diagonal across the bottom of the box:

$$120^2 + 90^2 = c^2$$ You might recognize this as a multiple of the common
$$14{,}400 + 8{,}100 = c^2$$ 3–4–5 right triangle.
$$c^2 = 22{,}500$$
$$c = 150$$

Next, find the diagonal of the rectangular box:

$$80^2 + 150^2 = c^2$$ You might recognize this as a multiple of the common
$$6{,}400 + 22{,}500 = c^2$$ 8–15–17 right triangle.
$$c^2 = 28{,}900$$
$$c = 170$$

MANHATTAN
PREP

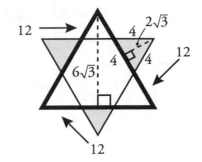

13. **$48\sqrt{3}$ cm²:** You can think of this star as a large equilateral triangle with sides 12 centimeters long, and three additional smaller equilateral triangles (shaded in the figure to the right) with sides 4 centimeters long. Using the same 30–60–90 logic discussed in chapter 4, note that the height of the larger equilateral triangle is $6\sqrt{3}$ and the height of the smaller equilateral triangle is $2\sqrt{3}$. Therefore, the areas of the triangles are as follows:

Large triangle: $A = \dfrac{b \times h}{2} = \dfrac{12 \times 6\sqrt{3}}{2} = 36\sqrt{3}$

Small triangles: $A = \dfrac{b \times h}{2} = \dfrac{4 \times 2\sqrt{3}}{2} = 4\sqrt{3}$

The total area of three smaller triangles and one large triangle is:

$36\sqrt{3} + 3(4\sqrt{3}) = 48\sqrt{3}$ cm²

Alternatively, you can apply the formula $A = \dfrac{S^2\sqrt{3}}{4}$:

Large triangle: $A = \dfrac{12^2\sqrt{3}}{4} = \dfrac{144\sqrt{3}}{4} = 36\sqrt{3}$

Small triangle: $A = \dfrac{4^2\sqrt{3}}{4} = \dfrac{16\sqrt{3}}{4} = 4\sqrt{3}$

Next, add the area of the large triangle and the area of three smaller triangles, as above.

14. **24 units:** The surface area of a cylinder is the area of the circular top and bottom, plus the area of its wrapped-around rectangular third face. You can express this in formula form as:

$SA = 2(\pi r^2) + 2\pi rh$

Substitute the known values into this formula to find the radius of the circular base:

$360\pi = 2(\pi r^2) + 2\pi r(3)$
$360\pi = 2\pi r^2 + 6\pi r$
$r^2 + 3r - 180 = 0$
$(r + 15)(r - 12) = 0$

$r + 15 = 0$ OR $r - 12 = 0$
$r = \{-15, 12\}$

Use only the positive value of r: 12. If $r = 12$, the diameter of the cylinder's circular base is 24.

7

15. **4π:** If the area of the circle is 81π, then the radius of the circle is 9 ($A = \pi r^2$). Therefore, the total circumference of the circle is 18π ($C = 2\pi r$). Angle ABC, an inscribed angle of 40°, corresponds to a central angle of 80°. Thus, arc AXC is equal to $\dfrac{80}{360} = \dfrac{2}{9}$ of the total circumference. Therefore, arc AXC equals $\dfrac{2}{9}(18\pi) = 4\pi$.

Appendix A

of Geometry

Data Sufficiency

In This Chapter...

Appendix A
Data Sufficiency

Data Sufficiency (DS) problems are a cross between math and logic. Imagine that your boss just walked into your office and dumped a bunch of papers on your desk, saying, "Hey, our client wants to know whether they should raise the price on this product. Can you answer that question from this data? If so, which pieces do we need to prove the case?" What would you do?

The client has asked a specific question: should the company raise the price? You have to decide which pieces of information will allow you to answer that question—or, possibly, that you don't have enough information to answer the question at all.

This kind of logical reasoning is exactly what you use when you answer DS questions.

How Data Sufficiency Works

If you already feel comfortable with the basics of Data Sufficiency, you may want to move quickly through this particular section of the chapter—but you are encouraged to read it. There are a few insights that you may find useful.

Every DS problem has the same basic form:

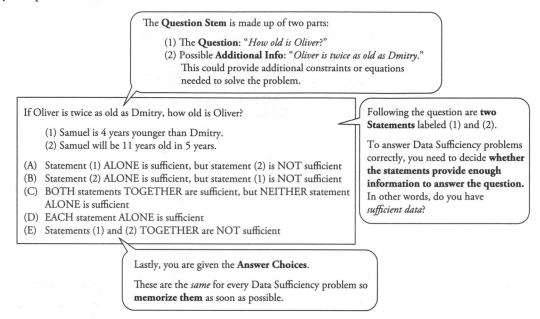

The **Question Stem** is made up of two parts:

(1) The **Question**: "*How old is Oliver?*"
(2) Possible **Additional Info**: "*Oliver is twice as old as Dmitry.*" This could provide additional constraints or equations needed to solve the problem.

If Oliver is twice as old as Dmitry, how old is Oliver?

    (1) Samuel is 4 years younger than Dmitry.
    (2) Samuel will be 11 years old in 5 years.

(A)   Statement (1) ALONE is sufficient, but statement (2) is NOT sufficient
(B)   Statement (2) ALONE is sufficient, but statement (1) is NOT sufficient
(C)   BOTH statements TOGETHER are sufficient, but NEITHER statement ALONE is sufficient
(D)   EACH statement ALONE is sufficient
(E)   Statements (1) and (2) TOGETHER are NOT sufficient

Following the question are **two Statements** labeled (1) and (2).

To answer Data Sufficiency problems correctly, you need to decide **whether the statements provide enough information to answer the question.** In other words, do you have *sufficient data?*

Lastly, you are given the **Answer Choices**.

These are the *same* for every Data Sufficiency problem so **memorize them** as soon as possible.

The question stem contains the question you need to answer. The two statements provide *given* information, information that is true. DS questions look strange but you can think of them as deconstructed Problem Solving (PS) questions. Compare the DS-format problem above to the PS-format problem below:

> Samuel is 4 years younger than Dmitry, and Samuel will be 11 years old in 5 years.
> If Oliver is twice as old as Dmitry, how old is Oliver?"

The two questions contain exactly the same information; that information is just presented in a different order. The PS question stem contains all of the givens as well as the question. The DS problem moves some of the givens down to statement (1) and statement (2).

As with regular PS problems, the given information in the DS statements is always true. In addition, the two statements won't contradict each other. In the same way that a PS question wouldn't tell you that $x > 0$ *and* $x < 0$, the two DS statements won't do that either.

In the PS format, you would go ahead and calculate Oliver's age. The DS format works a bit differently. Here is the full problem, including the answer choices:

> If Oliver is twice as old as Dmitry, how old is Oliver?
>
> (1) Samuel is 4 years younger than Dmitry.
> (2) Samuel will be 11 years old in 5 years.
>
> (A) Statement (1) ALONE is sufficient, but statement (2) is NOT sufficient.
> (B) Statement (2) ALONE is sufficient, but statement (1) is NOT sufficient.
> (C) BOTH statements TOGETHER are sufficient, but NEITHER statement ALONE is sufficient.
> (D) EACH statement ALONE is sufficient.
> (E) Statements (1) and (2) TOGETHER are NOT sufficient.

Despite all appearances, the question is not actually asking you to calculate Oliver's age. Rather, it's asking *which pieces of information* would allow you to calculate Oliver's age.

You may already be able solve this one on your own, but you'll see much harder problems on the test, so your first task is to learn how to work through DS questions in a systematic, consistent way.

As you think the problem through, jot down information from the question stem:

```
O age = ____ ?
  O = 2D
```

Hmm. If they tell you Dmitry's age, then you can find Oliver's age. Remember that!

Take a look at the first statement. Also, write down the $\frac{AD}{BCE}$ answer grid (you'll learn why as you work through the problem):

> (1) Samuel is 4 years younger than Dmitry.

```
O age = ____ ?      AD
  O = 2D            BCE
(1) S = D-4   | (2)
              |
              |
```

The first statement doesn't allow you to figure out anyone's real age. Statement (1), then, is *not sufficient*. Now you can cross off the top row of answers, (A) and (D).

Why? Here's the text for answers (A) and (D):

> (A) Statement (1) ALONE is sufficient, but statement (2) is NOT sufficient.
> (D) EACH statement ALONE is sufficient.

Both answers indicate that statement (1) is sufficient to answer the question. Because statement (1) is *not* sufficient to find Oliver's age, both (A) and (D) are wrong.

The answer choices will always appear in the order shown for the above problem, so any time you decide that statement (1) is not sufficient, you will always cross off answers (A) and (D). That's why your answer grid groups these two answers together.

Next, consider statement (2), but remember one tricky thing: forget what statement (1) told you. Because of the way DS is constructed, you must evaluate the two statements separately before you look at them together:

(2) Samuel will be 11 years old in 5 years.

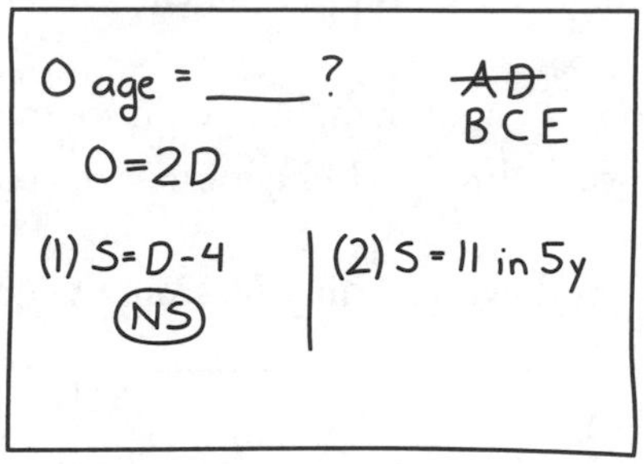

It's useful to write the two statements side-by-side, as shown above, to help remember that statement (2) is separate from statement (1) and has to be considered by itself first.

Statement (2) does indicate how old Sam is now, but says nothing about Oliver or Dmitry. (Remember, you're looking *only* at statement (2) now.) By itself, statement (2) is not sufficient, so cross off answer (B).

Now that you've evaluated each statement by itself, take a look at the two statements together. Statement (2) provides Sam's age, and statement (1) allows you to calculate Dmitry's age if you know Sam's age. Finally, the question stem allows you to calculate Oliver's age if you know Dmitry's age:

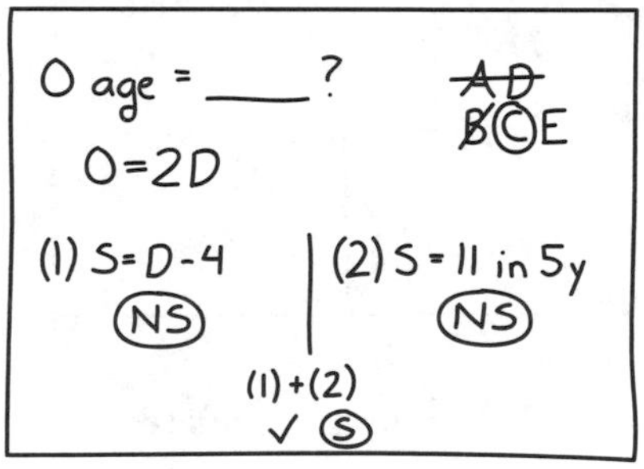

As soon as you can tell that you *can* solve, put down a check mark or write an S with a circle around it (or both!). Don't actually calculate Oliver's age; the GMAT doesn't give you any extra time to calculate a number that you don't need.

The correct answer is **(C)**.

The Answer Choices

The five Data Sufficiency answer choices will always be exactly the same (and presented in the same order), so memorize them before you go into the test.

Here are the five answers written in an easier way to understand:

(A) Statement (1) does allow you to answer the question, but statement (2) does not.
(B) Statement (2) does allow you to answer the question, but statement (1) does not.
(C) Neither statement works on its own, but you can use them *together* to answer the question.
(D) Statement (1) works by itself *and* statement (2) works by itself.
(E) Nothing works. Even if you use both statements together, you still can't answer the question.

Answer (C) specifically says that neither statement works on its own. For this reason, you are required to look at each statement by itself *and decide that neither one works* before you are allowed to evaluate the two statements together.

Here's an easier way to remember the five answer choices; we call this the "twelve-ten" mnemonic (memory aid):

1	only statement 1
2	only statement 2
T	together
E	either one
N	neither/nothing

Within the next week, memorize the DS answers. If you do a certain number of practice DS problems in that time frame, you'll likely memorize the answers without conscious effort—and you'll solidify the DS lessons you're learning right now.

Starting with Statement (2)

If statement (1) looks hard, start with statement (2) instead. Your process will be the same, except you'll make one change in your answer grid.

Try this problem:

If Oliver is twice as old as Dmitry, how old is Oliver?

(1) Two years ago, Dmitry was twice as old as Samuel.
(2) Samuel is 6 years old.

(From now on, the answer choices won't be shown. Start memorizing!)

Statement (1) is definitely more complicated than statement (2), so start with statement (2) instead. Change your answer grid to $\frac{BD}{ACE}$. (You'll learn why in a minute.)

(2) Samuel is 6 years old.

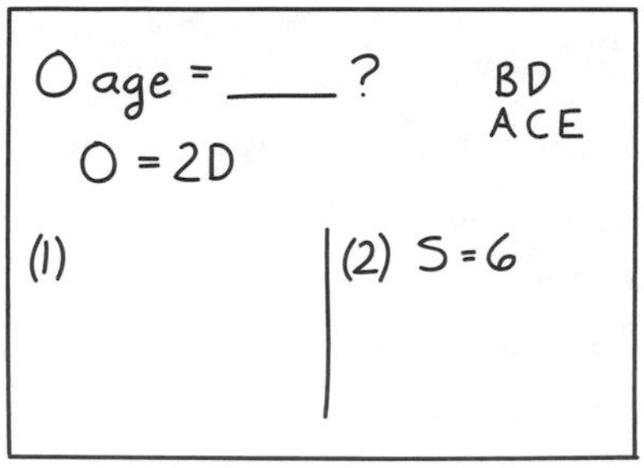

Statement (2) is not sufficient to determine Oliver's age, so cross off the answers that say statement (2) is sufficient: (B) and (D). Once again, you can cross off the entire top row; when starting with statement (2), you always will keep or eliminate these two choices at the same time.

Now assess statement (1):

(1) Two years ago, Dmitry was twice as old as Samuel.

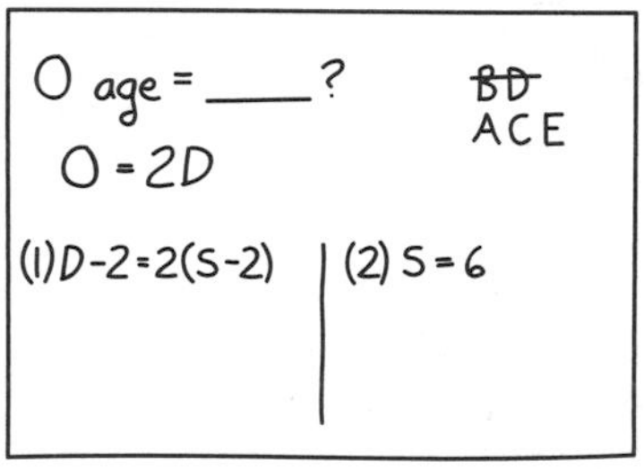

Forget all about statement (2); only statement (1) exists. By itself, is the statement sufficient?

Nope! Too many variables. Cross off (A), the first of the remaining answers in the bottom row, and assess the two statements together:

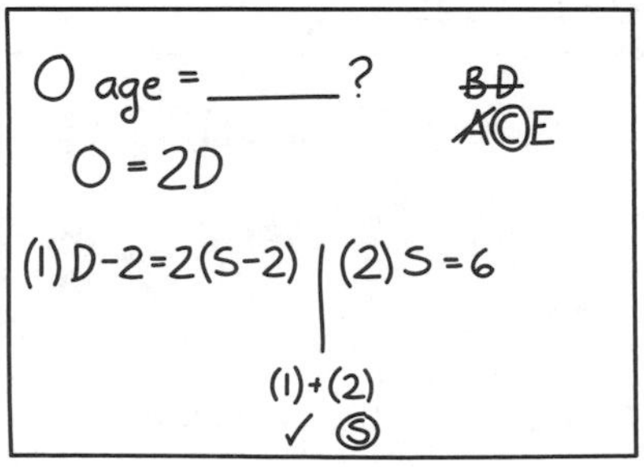

You can plug Samuel's age (from the second statement) into the formula from statement (1) to find Dmitry's age, and then use Dmitry's age to find Oliver's age. Together, the statements are sufficient.

The correct answer is **(C)**.

MANHATTAN
PREP

The two answer grids work in the same way, regardless of which one you use. As long as you use the AD/BCE grid when starting with statement (1), or the BD/ACE grid when starting with statement (2), you will always:

- cross off the *top* row if the first statement you try is *not* sufficient;

- cross off the *bottom* row if the first statement you try *is* sufficient; and

- assess the remaining row of answers one answer at a time.

Finally, remember that you must assess the statements separately before you can try them together—and you'll only try them together if neither one is sufficient on its own. You will only consider the two together if you have already crossed off answers (A), (B), and (D).

Value vs. Yes/No Questions

Data Sufficiency questions come in two "flavors": Value or Yes/No.

On Value questions, it is necessary to find a single value in order to answer the question. If you can't find any value or you can find two or more values, then the information is not sufficient.

Consider this statement:

> (1) Oliver's age is a multiple of 4.

Oliver could be 4 or 8 or 12 or any age that is a multiple of 4. Because it's impossible to determine one particular value for Oliver's age, the statement is not sufficient

What if the question changed?

> Is Oliver's age an even number?
>
> (1) Oliver's age is a multiple of 4.
> (2) Oliver is between 19 and 23 years old.

This question is a Yes/No question. There are three possible answers to a Yes/No question:

1. Always Yes: Sufficient!

2. Always No: Sufficient!

3. Maybe (or Sometimes Yes, Sometimes No): Not Sufficient

It may surprise you that Always No is sufficient to answer the question. Imagine that you ask a friend to go to the movies with you. If she says, "No, I'm sorry, I can't," then you did receive an answer to your question (even though the answer is negative). You know she can't go to the movies with you.

Apply this reasoning to the Oliver question. Is statement 1 sufficient to answer the question *Is Oliver's age an even number?*

> (1) Oliver's age is a multiple of 4.

If Oliver's age is a multiple of 4, then Yes, he must be an even number of years old. The information isn't enough to tell how old Oliver actually is—he could be 4, 8, 12, or any multiple of 4 years old. Still, the information is sufficient to answer the specific question asked.

Because the statement tried first is sufficient, cross off the bottom row of answers, (B), (C), and (E).

Next, check statement (2):

> (2) Oliver is between 19 and 23 years old.

Oliver could be 20, in which case his age is even. He could also be 21, in which case his age is odd. The answer here is Sometimes Yes, Sometimes No, so the information is not sufficient to answer the question.

The correct answer is **(A)**: the first statement is sufficient but the second is not.

The DS Process

This section summarizes everything you've learned in one consistent DS process. You can use this on every DS problem on the test.

Step 1: Determine whether the question is Value or Yes/No.

Value: The question asks for the value of an unknown (e.g., What is x?).

> A statement is **Sufficient** when it provides **1 possible value**.

> A statement is **Not Sufficient** when it provides **more than 1 possible value** (or none at all).

Yes/No: The question asks whether a given piece of information is true (e.g., Is x even?). Most of the time, these will be in the form of Yes/No questions.

> A statement is **Sufficient** when the answer is **Always Yes** or **Always No**.

> A statement is **Not Sufficient** when the answer is **Maybe** or **Sometimes Yes, Sometimes No**.

Step 2: Separate given information from the question itself.

If the question stem contains given information—that is, any information other than the question itself—then write down that information separately from the question itself. This is true information that you must consider or use when answering the question.

Step 3: Rephrase the question.

Most of the time, you will not write down the entire question stem exactly as it appears on screen. At the least, you'll simplify what is written on screen. For example, if the question stem asks, "What is the value of x?" then you might write down something like $x =$ _____ ?

For more complicated question stems, you may have more work to do. Ideally, before you go to the statements, you will be able to articulate a fairly clear and straightforward question. In the earlier example, $x =$ _____ ? is clear and straightforward.

What if this is the question?

If $xyz \neq 0$, is $\dfrac{3x}{2} + y + 2z = \dfrac{7x}{2} + y$?

(1) $y = 3$ and $x = 2$
(2) $z = -x$

Do you need to know the individual values of x, y, and z in order to answer the question? Would knowing the value of a combination of the variables, such as $x + y + z$, work? It's tough to tell.

In order to figure this out, **rephrase** the question stem, which is a fancy way of saying: simplify the information a lot. Take the time to do this before you address the statements; you'll make your job much easier!

If you're given an equation, the first task is to put the "like" variables together. Also, when working with the question stem, make sure to carry the question mark through your work:

$$y - y + 2z = \dfrac{7x}{2} - \dfrac{3x}{2}?$$

That's interesting: the two y variables cancel out. Keep simplifying:

$$2z = \dfrac{4x}{2}?$$
$$2z = 2x?$$
$$z = x?$$

That whole crazy equation is really asking a much simpler question: is $z = x$?

It might seem silly to keep writing that question mark at the end of each line, but don't skip that step or you'll be opening yourself up to a careless error. By the time you get to the end, you don't want to forget that this is still a *question*, not a statement or given.

Step 4: Use the Answer Grid to Evaluate the Statements

If you start with statement 1, then write the AD/BCE grid on your scrap paper.

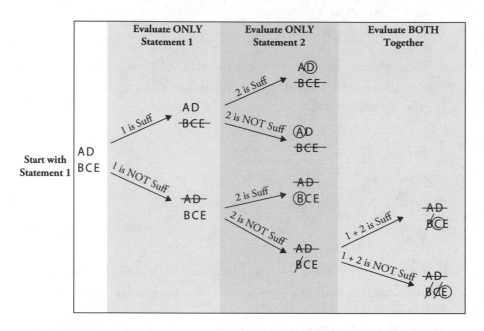

Here is the rephrased problem:

> If $xyz \neq 0$, is $z = x$?
>
> (1) $y = 3$ and $x = 2$
> (2) $z = -x$

Statement (1) is useless by itself because it says nothing about z. Cross off the top row of answers: $\dfrac{\text{AD}}{\text{BCE}}$

Statement (2) turns out to be very useful. None of the variables is 0, so if $z = -x$, then those two numbers cannot be equal to each other. This statement is sufficient to answer the question: no, z does not equal x. You can circle B on your grid: $\dfrac{\text{AD}}{\text{BCE}}$

The correct answer is (**B**).

If you decide to start with statement (2), your process is almost identical, but you'll use the BD/ACE grid instead. For example:

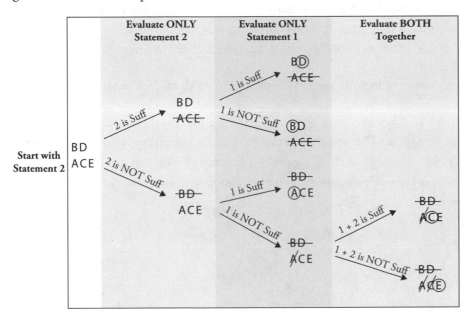

First, evaluate statement (1) by itself and, if you've crossed off answers (A), (B), and (D), then evaluate the two statements together.

Whether you use AD/BCE or BD/ACE, remember to

- cross off the *top* row if the first statement you try is *not* sufficient, and
- cross off the *bottom* row if the first statement you try *is* sufficient.

Pop Quiz! Test Your Skills

Have you learned the DS process? If not, go back through the chapter and work through the sample problems again. Try writing out each step yourself.

If so, prove it! Give yourself up to four minutes total to try the following two problems:

1. Are there more engineers than salespeople working at SoHo Corp?

    (1) SoHo Corp employs $\frac{2}{3}$ as many clerical staff as engineers and salespeople combined.
    (2) If 3 more engineers were employed by SoHo Corp and the number of salespeople remained the same, then the number of engineers would be double the number of salespeople employed by the company.

2. At SoHo Corp, what is the ratio of managers to non-managers?

   (1) If there were 3 more managers and the number of salespeople remained the
       same, then the ratio of managers to non-managers would double.
   (2) There are 4 times as many non-managers as managers at SoHo Corp.

How did it go? Are you very confident in your answers? Somewhat confident? Not at all confident?

Before you check your answers, go back over your work, using the DS process discussed in this chapter as your guide. Where can you improve? Did you write down (and use!) your answer grid? Did you look at each statement separately before looking at them together (if necessary)? Did you mix up any of the steps of the process? How neat is the work on your scrap paper? You may want to rewrite your work before you review the answers.

Pop Quiz Answer Key

1. Engineers vs. Salespeople

Step 1: Is this a Value or Yes/No question?

   1. Are there more engineers than salespeople working at SoHo Corp?

This is a Yes/No question.

Steps 2 and 3: What is given and what is the question? Rephrase the question.

The question stem doesn't contain any given information. In this case, the question is already about as simplified as it can get: are there more engineers than salespeople?

Step 4: Evaluate the statements.

If you start with the first statement, use the AD/BCE answer grid.

   (1) SoHo Corp employs $\frac{2}{3}$ as many clerical staff as engineers and salespeople combined.

If you add up the engineers and salespeople, then there are fewer people on the clerical staff...but this indicates nothing about the relative number of engineers and salespeople. This statement is not sufficient. Cross off (A) and (D), the top row, of your answer grid.

   (2) If 3 more engineers were employed by SoHo Corp and the number of salespeople
       remained the same, then the number of engineers would be double the number of
       salespeople employed by the company.

This one sounds promising. If you add only 3 engineers, then you'll have twice as many engineers as salespeople. Surely, that means there are more engineers than salespeople?

Don't jump to any conclusions. Test some possible numbers; think about fairly extreme scenarios. What if you start with just 1 engineer? When you add 3, you'll have 4 engineers. If there are 4 engineers, then there are half as many, or 2, salespeople. In other words, you start with 1 engineer and 2 salespeople, so there are more salespeople. Interesting.

According to this one case, the answer to the Yes/No question *Are there more engineers than salespeople?* is no.

Can you find a yes answer? Try a larger set of numbers. If you start with 11 engineers and add 3, then you would have 14 total. The number of salespeople would have to be 7. In this case, then, there are more engineers to start than salespeople, so the answer to the question *Are there more engineers than salespeople?* is yes.

Because you can find both yes and no answers, statement (2) is not sufficient. Cross off answer (B).

Now, try the two statements together. How does the information about the clerical staff combine with statement (2)?

Whenever you're trying some numbers and you have to examine the two statements together, see whether you can reuse the numbers that you tried earlier.

If you start with 1 engineer, you'll have 2 salespeople, for a total of 3. In this case, you'd have 2 clerical staff, and the answer to the original question is no.

If you start with 11 engineers, you'll have 7 salespeople, for a total of 18. In this case, you'd have 12 clerical staff, and the answer to the original question is yes.

The correct answer is **(E)**. The information is not sufficient even when both statements are used together.

2. Managers vs. Non-Managers

Step 1: Is this a Value or a Yes/No question?

>   2. At SoHo Corp, what is the ratio of managers to non-managers?

This is a Value question. You need to find one specific ratio—or know that you can find one specific ratio—in order to answer the question.

Steps 2 and 3: What is given and what is the question? Rephrase the question.

Find the ratio of managers to non-managers, or $M : N$.

Step 4: Evaluate the statements.

If you start with the second statement, use the BD/ACE answer grid. (Note: this is always your choice; the solution with the BD/ACE grid shown is just for practice.)

(2) There are 4 times as many non-managers as managers at SoHo Corp.

If there is 1 manager, there are 4 non-managers. If there are 2 managers, there are 8 non-managers. If there are 3 managers, there are 12 non-managers.

What does that mean? In each case, the ratio of managers to non-managers is the same, 1 : 4. Even though you don't know how many managers and non-managers there are, you do know the ratio. (For more on ratios, see the Ratios chapter of the *Fractions, Decimals, & Percents GMAT Strategy Guide*.)

This statement is sufficient; cross (A), (C), and (E), the bottom row, off of the grid.

(1) If there were 3 more managers and the number of salespeople remained the same, then the ratio of managers to non-managers would double.

First, what does it mean to *double* a ratio? If the starting ratio were 2 : 3, then doubling that ratio would give you 4 : 3. The first number in the ratio doubles relative to the second number.

Test some cases. If you start with 1 manager, then 3 more would bring the total number of managers to 4. The *manager* part of the ratio just quadrupled (1 to 4), not doubled, so this number is not a valid starting point. Discard this case.

If you have to add 3 and want that number to double, then you need to start with 3 managers. When you add 3 more, that portion of the ratio doubles from 3 to 6. The other portion, the non-managers, remains the same.

Notice anything? The statement says nothing about the relative number of non-managers. The starting ratio could be 3 : 2 or 3 : 4 or 3 : 14, for all you know. In each case, doubling the number of managers would double the ratio (to 6 : 2, or 6 : 4, or 6 : 14). You can't figure out the specific ratio from this statement.

The correct answer is **(B)**: statement (2) is sufficient, but statement (1) is not.

Proving Insufficiency

The Pop Quiz solutions used the Testing Cases strategy: testing real numbers to help determine whether a statement is sufficient. You can do this whenever the problem allows for the possibility of multiple numbers or cases.

When you're doing this, your goal is to try to prove the statement insufficient. For example:

> If x and y are positive integers, is the sum of x and y between 20 and 26, inclusive?

> (1) $x - y = 6$

Test your first case. You're allowed to pick any numbers for x and y that make statement 1 true *and* that follow any constraints given in the question stem. In this case, that means the two numbers have to be positive integers and that $x - y$ has to equal 6.

Case #1: $20 - 14 = 6$. These numbers make statement 1 true and follow the constraint in the question stem, so these are legal numbers to pick. Now, try to answer the Yes/No question: $20 + 14 = 34$, so no, the sum is not between 20 and 26, inclusive.

You now have a *no* answer. Can you think of another set of numbers that will give you the opposite, a *yes* answer?

Case #2: $15 - 9 = 6$. In this case, the sum is 24, so the answer to the Yes/No question is yes, the sum is between 20 and 26, inclusive.

Because you have found both a yes and a no answer, the statement is not sufficient.

Here's a summary of the process:

1. Notice that you can test cases. You can do this when the problem allows for multiple possible values.

2. Pick numbers that make the statement true and that follow any givens in the question stem. If you realize that you picked numbers that make the statement false or contradict givens in the question stem, *discard* those numbers and start over.

3. Your first case will give you one answer: a yes or a no on a Yes/No problem, or a numerical value on a value problem.

4. Try to find a second case that gives you a *different* answer. On a Yes/No problem, you'll be looking for the opposite of what you found for the first case. For a Value problem, you'll be looking for a different numerical answer. (Don't forget that whatever you pick still has to make the statement true and follow the givens in the question stem!)

The usefulness of trying to prove insufficiency is revealed as soon as you find two different answers. You're done! That statement is not sufficient, so you can cross off an answer or answers and move to the next step.

What if you keep finding the same answer? Try this:

> If *x* and *y* are positive integers, is the product of *x* and *y* between 20 and 26, inclusive?
>
> (1) *x* is a multiple of 17.

Case #1: Test $x = 17$. Since *y* must be a positive integer, try the smallest possible value first: $y = 1$. In this case, the product is 17, which is not between 20 and 26 inclusive. The answer to the question is *no*; can you find the opposite answer?

Case #2: If you make $x = 34$, then *xy* will be too big, so keep $x = 17$. The next smallest possible value for *y* is 2. In this case, the product is 34, which is also not between 20 and 26 inclusive. The answer is again no.

Can you think of a case where you will get a *yes* answer? No! The smallest possible product is 17, and the next smallest possible product is 34. Any additional values of *x* and *y* you try will be equal to or larger than 34.

You've just proved the statement sufficient because it is impossible to find a yes answer. Testing Cases can help you to figure out the "theory" answer, or the mathematical reasoning that proves the statement is sufficient.

This won't always work so cleanly. Sometimes, you'll keep getting all no answers or all yes answers but you won't be able to figure out the theory behind it all. If you test three or four different cases, and you're actively seeking out the opposite answer but never find it, then go ahead and assume that the statement is sufficient, even if you're not completely sure why.

Do make sure that you're trying numbers with different characteristics. Try both even and odd. Try a prime number. Try zero or a negative or a fraction. (You can only try numbers that are allowed by the problem, of course. In the case of the above problems, you were only allowed to try positive integers.)

Here's how Testing Cases would work on a Value problem:

> If *x* and *y* are prime numbers, what is the product of *x* and *y*?
>
> (1) The product is even.

Case #1: $x = 2$ and $y = 3$. Both numbers are prime numbers and their product is even, so these are legal numbers to try. In this case, the product is 6. Can you choose numbers that will give a different product?

Case #2: $x = 2$ and $y = 5$. Both numbers are prime numbers and their product is even, so these are legal numbers to try. In this case, the product is 10.

The statement is not sufficient because there are at least two different values for the product of x and y.

In short, when you're evaluating DS statements, go into them with an "I'm going to try to prove you insufficient!" mindset.

- If you do find two different answers (yes and no, or two different numbers), then immediately declare that statement not sufficient.

- If, after several tries, you keep finding the same answer despite trying different kinds of numbers, see whether you can articulate why; that statement may be sufficient after all. Even if you can't say why, go ahead and assume that the statement is sufficient.

Now you're ready to test your Data Sufficiency skills. As you work through the chapters in this book, test your progress using some of the *Official Guide* problem set lists found online, in your Manhattan Prep Student Center. Start with lower-numbered problems first, in order to practice the process, and work your way up to more and more difficult problems.

Geometry Cheat Sheet

Shown on the reverse. Feel free to cut or tear out this page to keep as a reference.

Area

$A = s^2$

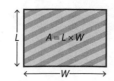
$A = L \times W$

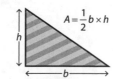
$A = \frac{1}{2} b \times h$

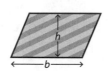
$A = \frac{1}{2} b \times h$

$A = \left(\frac{b_1 + b_2}{2} \right) \times h$

$A = b \times h$

Perimeter

P = 4x

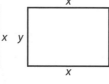
P = 2x + 2y

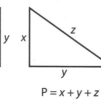
P = x + y + z

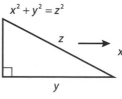
P = 2x + 2y

Special Right Triangles

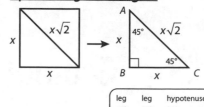

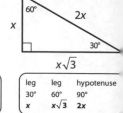

leg	leg	hypotenuse
45°	45°	90°
x	**x**	**x√2**

leg	leg	hypotenuse
30°	60°	90°
x	**x√3**	**2x**

Triangles

$x^2 + y^2 = z^2$ → $z = \sqrt{x^2 + y^2}$

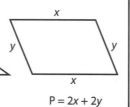

Pythagorean Triplets
3–4–5
6–8–10
5–12–13
8–15–17

$a° > b° > c° \leftrightarrow x > y > z$

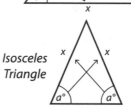

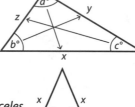

Similar Triangles

$\frac{a}{d} = \frac{b}{e} = \frac{c}{f}$

Isosceles Triangle

Circles

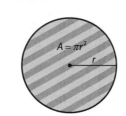
$A = \pi r^2$

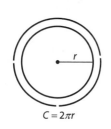
$C = 2\pi r$

Inscribed Angles

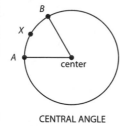
CENTRAL ANGLE

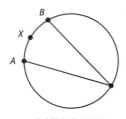
INSCRIBED ANGLE

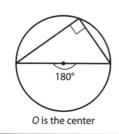
180°

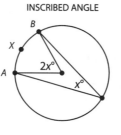
O is the center

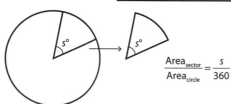

$$\frac{\text{Area}_{\text{sector}}}{\text{Area}_{\text{circle}}} = \frac{s}{360}$$

3-D Shapes

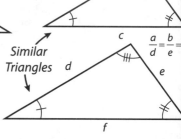

Volume $= l \times w \times h$
Surface Area $= 2 \times (l \times w + l \times h + w \times h)$

Volume $= s^3$
Surface Area $= 6s^2$

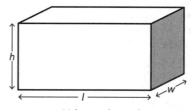
Volume $= \pi r^2 h$
Surface Area $= 2(\pi r^2) + 2\pi rh$

Slopes

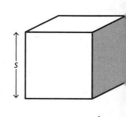

$\frac{-}{+} =$ negative

$\frac{+}{+} =$ positive

$\frac{0}{+} = 0$

$\frac{+}{0} =$ undefined

Coordinate Plane

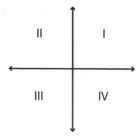

II	I
III	IV

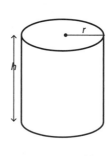

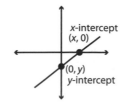
x-intercept (x, 0)
(0, y) y-intercept

slope $= \frac{y_2 - y_1}{x_2 - x_1}$ or $\frac{y_1 - y_2}{x_1 - x_2}$

$y = mx + b$

slope, y-intercept

slopes of perpendicular lines:
negative reciprocals

ex. l_1 slope $= \frac{1}{2}$, l_2 slope $= -2$

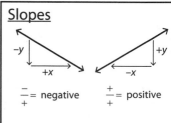

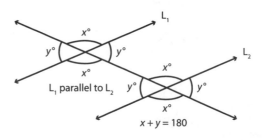
L_1 parallel to L_2
$x + y = 180$

GO BEYOND BOOKS.
TRY A FREE CLASS NOW.

IN-PERSON COURSE

Find a GMAT course near you and attend the first session free, no strings attached. You'll meet your instructor, learn how the GMAT is scored, review strategies for Data Sufficiency, dive into Sentence Correction, and gain insights into a wide array of GMAT principles and strategies.

Find your city at manhattanprep.com/gmat/classes

ONLINE COURSE

Enjoy the flexibility of prepping from home or the office with our online course. Your instructor will cover all the same content and strategies as an in-person course, while giving you the freedom to prep where you want. Attend the first session free to check out our cutting-edge online classroom.

See the full schedule at manhattanprep.com/gmat/classes

GMAT® INTERACT™

GMAT Interact is a comprehensive self-study program that is fun, intuitive, and driven by you. Each interactive video lesson is taught by an expert instructor and can be accessed on your computer or mobile device. Lessons are personalized for you based on the choices you make.

Try 5 full lessons for free at manhattanprep.com/gmat/interact

Not sure which is right for you? Try all three! Or give us a call and we'll help you figure out which program fits you best.

Toll-Free U.S. Number (800) 576-4628 | **International** 001 (212) 721-7400 | **Email** gmat@manhattanprep.com

mbaMission

PREP MADE PERSONAL

Whether you want quick coaching in a particular GMAT subject area or a comprehensive study plan developed around your goals, we've got you covered. Our expert, 99th percentile GMAT tutors can help you hit your top score.

CHECK OUT THESE REVIEWS FROM MANHATTAN PREP TUTORING STUDENTS.

CALL OR EMAIL US AT **800-576-4628** OR **GMAT@MANHATTANPREP.COM** FOR INFORMATION ON RATES AND TO GET PAIRED WITH YOUR GMAT TUTOR.